Ferdinand S. Mathews

Familiar Life in Field and Forest

The animals, birds, frogs, and salamanders

Ferdinand S. Mathews

Familiar Life in Field and Forest
The animals, birds, frogs, and salamanders

ISBN/EAN: 9783337096823

Printed in Europe, USA, Canada, Australia, Japan

Cover: Foto ©Andreas Hilbeck / pixelio.de

More available books at **www.hansebooks.com**

YOUNG FOXES.
Painted by F. Schuyler Mathews from a photograph by W. Lyman Underwood.

FAMILIAR LIFE IN FIELD AND FOREST

※　※　※

THE · ANIMALS · BIRDS FROGS · AND · SALAMANDERS

BY

F. SCHUYLER MATHEWS

AUTHOR OF FAMILIAR FLOWERS OF FIELD AND GARDEN,
FAMILIAR TREES AND THEIR LEAVES, FAMILIAR FEATURES
OF THE ROADSIDE, THE BEAUTIFUL FLOWER GARDEN, ETC.

*WITH NUMEROUS ILLUSTRATIONS BY
THE AUTHOR, AND PHOTOGRAPHS FROM
NATURE BY W. LYMAN UNDERWOOD*

NEW YORK
D. APPLETON AND COMPANY
1898

PREFACE.

There are few things more gratifying to the lover of Nature than those momentary glimpses of wild life which he obtains while passing through the field or forest. Wild animals do not confine themselves exclusively to the wilderness; quite frequently they venture upon the highway, and we are apt to regard the meeting with one of them there as a rare and fortunate occurrence.

The daisy and the wild rose appear in their appointed places on the return of summer, and the song sparrow sings in the same tree he frequented the year before; but the woodchuck, the raccoon, and the deer are not so often found exactly where we think they belong. To seek an interview with such wild folk is like taking a chance in a lottery: there are numerous blanks and but few prizes.

But because wild life is not in constant evidence, like the wild flower, is no proof that it is uncommon. To those who keep in touch with Nature it becomes

a very familiar thing, and to live a while where the
wild creatures make their homes is to cross their
paths continually.   I have not failed to meet that
much-slandered animal, the skunk, every summer for
seven years past, yet with no unhappy results; I have
haunted a fox's hole the better part of one season,
and have evidently crossed his freshly made tracks,
but with not one lucky chance at the sight of him;
yet when I had no thought of Reynard and was
searching the woods for the *Cypripedium*, there he
was!   On another occasion he was unexpectedly en-
countered in the open pasture by some of the members of the household, and still later he was seen
seated on the highway not very far from the pet cat.

One can never tell at what moment some surprising demonstration of wild life will occur at one's very
doorstep.   What with two deer, nine weasels, and a
performing bear, all of which appeared in one day
last summer close to my studio, I concluded that our
tame mountain retreat had relapsed again to the wild
and happy conditions of the primitive forest.   But I
was forced to change my mind a few days after, when
an Italian with his organ ground out "Johnny, get
your gun" within forty feet of the spot where the
wild deer had stood.

It may be largely a matter of good fortune if one
catches a glimpse of some wild creature of the woods

in the way I have just described; but in the forest it unquestionably depends upon the skillful movements and quiet demeanor of the observer that he can see without being seen. The wild animals never become familiar to one who is heedless and impatient. The waggle of a leaf or the snapping of a twig sends the timid burrower to the depths of his hole, and it requires more than the patience of Job to await his reappearance. It is necessary to count time by heart-throbs rather than seconds when one enters the woodland; indeed, it is possibly better to take no account of it at all, but lavish it generously upon chances. Perhaps such an apparent waste of time would be called loafing; if so, then Thoreau was a magnificent loafer. But loafers do not bequeath to us a world of woodland knowledge such as Thoreau did.

We are at fault because we do not enter the wood and do a little thinking on our own account. Perhaps if we did we would discover that the deer, the marten, the loon, and the bear were not half so uncommon as we thought they were. Nor can we rely wholly upon what the books say. Audubon, Wilson, Rymer Jones, and Elliott Coues are all well enough in their way, but they smack somewhat of ancient history. The development of natural history in this country is of very recent date; one naturalist has informed me that up to about ten years ago one of the most remarkable and typical little mammals of Florida, a water rat (*Microtus neofiber allenii*), had absolutely no record whatever. In a pamphlet entitled The Land Mammals of Florida, by Mr. Outram Bangs (1898), of seventy-three forms described, seventeen are new. When Wilson wrote, in 1812, he knew positively nothing at all of the songs of the nightingale of America—the hermit thrush—and the veery, the thrush named for him! Even in so late a book as The Fur-bearing Animals of Elliott Coues, the European ermine is confused with two of our American weasels. Such an error as that in these days of greater light would be deemed inexcusable.

It is to some of the younger students of Nature that we are indebted for a more concise knowledge of the relationship of animals—in other words, the exact identification of distinct species and varieties. Dr. Merriam makes this fact plain in the following tribute to the work of Mr. Bangs. He says: "Until very recently the group of weasels has been in a state of chaos, but now, thanks to Mr. Outram Bangs's excellent paper entitled A Review of the Weasels of Eastern North America, the obscurity that has so long surrounded our Eastern species has been cleared away." *

---

* *Vide* United States Department of Agriculture, Division of Ornithology and Mammals. Bulletin No. 11, June, 1896.

There is more in a *name* in natural history than one would suppose. The change, in these latter days, of a Latin name generally means that the exact nature of the beast is at last discovered. For instance, the flying squirrel, *Sciuropterus sabrinus*, is a large, and in winter a distinctly yellow-tinged, gray-coated creature, whose white chest fur, if you blow it, is lead-colored at the base. The commoner species, *Sciuropterus volans volans*, is a different animal, whose under fur is quite white. Not many years ago these two squirrels were not distinguished apart and therefore were known by one name. To-day the old name for the Virginia deer, *Cariacus virginianus*, is displaced by the newer one, *Odocoileus virginianus*.* The recent change means that until this last winter (1898) this particular species has not been properly distinguished apart from other species.

But I can not lightly pass the old and inestimably valuable works of Audubon, Wilson, and Elliott Coues without a tribute to their excellence. These great naturalists were pioneers, and all they have to say is worthy of the closest study; consequently I have freely quoted such passages from their works as I considered would throw a strong light on the sub-

---

* *Vide* Proceedings of the Biological Society of Washington, p. 99, 1898.

ject. Regarding Dr. Clinton Hart Merriam's Animals of the Adirondacks, I can only add that I consider it a classic, and until some writer shall exceed its simple and attractive presentation of important facts, it must be regarded, as far as it goes, as the best biography of American animals which we to-day possess.

It should be borne in mind that the times change, a scientific knowledge of animals grows, and the wild creatures themselves shift their position over the land. What was supposed to be uncommon or extinct twenty years ago can not be regarded so to-day. The borders of abandoned farms are constantly—not rarely—invaded by animals who were not supposed to live within miles of the old places. Occasionally an otter, a lynx, a deer, or a bear turns up most unexpectedly, and immediately all the country turns out to hunt the creature down.

Unfortunately, we have no proper appreciation of the inherent good in a wild animal; one would think, by the way men acted, that it had no right to live. There is no logical reason why we should slay a snake, skunk, fox, weasel or raccoon unless it becomes a public nuisance and we are compelled to put an end to its depredations.

There is something satisfactory in the feeling of our own harmlessness in the presence of some poor

frightened creature whose wild eyes betray the fear
that we are a deadly enemy; and with what comfort-
ing assurance we hasten to say, " No, you are greatly
mistaken, I bear you no ill; I am your friend." If
only the poor thing could *know* that, how much hap-
pier the world would wag on!

One feels just a bit of exultant pleasure when one
sees the little wild thing approach, timidly accept a
proffered nut or a crust of bread, and actually eat it
within reaching distance. I recall with no small
feeling of satisfaction the time when, idly paddling
my canoe beside the   river bank, I met
a great blue heron slow-   ly strolling
along the sandy margin,   and
remained beside him for fully
twenty minutes an acceptable companion. Nor do I forget the time
when I approached, softly whistling the
while, a brown heron standing motionless on the meadow, and got so near him
that I could see the round shape of his eye as plainly as I have drawn it here. There is a certain
charm in music for the wild animals. I have whistled by the half hour to the hermit thrush and have
received an appreciative and cordial response; the
veery grows quite excited if I imitate his spiral
song; the red squirrel sits transfixed if I play for

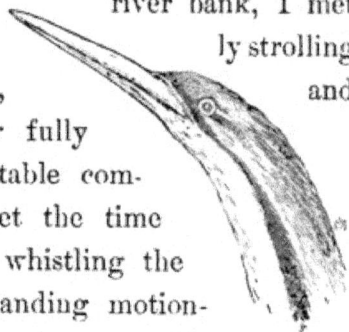

FAMILIAR LIFE IN FIELD AND FOREST.

him on an insignificant ten-cent harmonicon. One time I noticed a particularly vociferous fellow subside, cross his hands on his breast, and listen respectfully to the soothing strains of " Home, sweet home."

All this goes to prove that the wild life of the woods is not unapproachable. It may be difficult to cultivate its friendship, but it responds. It is an easy matter to pick a daisy and carelessly throw it away; but when we have persuaded a wild bird or a squirrel to eat from our hand, we never throw the memory of that away: it abides with us forever!

Guns and traps are all very well in their way, but a conscience void of offense to the animal world is better. There never was a world more peculiarly beset with enemies of all kinds and degrees than the wild animal world; it has to make a fight of life, anyway; and then there is the common enemy, man, to reckon with, who crushes the snake, hunts the fox and bear, worries the woodchuck, shoots the bird, traps the marten, kills the deer, and makes war generally upon all wild life without discrimination. One of these days, when the cutworm, the grasshopper, the field mouse, the army worm, and the gypsy moth devour the farm, house and all, we will wonder what has become of the beneficent skunk, weasel, and snake. Perhaps we have yet time enough to give these poor creatures a chance to learn we are friends, and not enemies.

I have no excuse for these imperfect records of my own experience with wild animals except the one that I have lived long enough among them to respect their rights of life and speak a good word for them when occasion offers. There is only one creature I know of who seems to be a thoroughly ugly character, afflicted with a most uncontrollable and vicious temper—that is, the Injun Devil, or wild cat (*Lynx canadensis*). Fortunately, he rarely appears this side of the Canadian border; when he does, the hunter gives him no peace, for there *is* no peace where he exists.

I wish to add, that without the valuable assistance of Prof. Samuel Garman, Mr. Outram Bangs, and Mr. Samuel Henshaw, which I most gratefully acknowledge, I never would have been able to gather together the latest scientific facts regarding the animals. Also, the book would have lost much without Mr. W. Lyman Underwood's contribution of photographs from Nature. But the fact is, two heads are always better than one; and consequently the book, which is *not* the selfish outcome of one man's thoughts, escapes at least one fault—it is not one-sided.

F. Schuyler Mathews.

El Fureidis, Blair, Campton, N. H.,
May, 1898.

CONTENTS.

xiii

LIST OF FULL-PAGE ILLUSTRATIONS.

xvi   FAMILIAR LIFE IN FIELD AND FOREST.

FAMILIAR LIFE
IN FIELD AND FOREST.

CHAPTER I.

EARLY VOICES OF SPRING.

The Hyla, Acris, Chorophilus, and Bufo.

THE path that follows the course of the stream through the meadow is bordered with miniature leaflets which are growing rapidly in the sunbeams of early April. The young fuzzy leaves of the liverwort (*Hepatica triloba*) at our feet are in company with a few promising buds, but the old brown leaves that have survived the winter snows are still reluctant to give up life and let the younger generation carry it forward. The brook is rushing tumultuously toward the river, with no time to linger now in the pebbly depths where last August all was quiet, and the lazy trout scarcely moved his tail to keep his place under the sheltering bank. Farther along where the brook widens at the level of the river, in a snarl of freshet-dragged alders and willows, there is a muskrat busily engaged in gnawing a tender twig, all impatience and hurry; possibly the creature is building a nest. As we wander along a little farther a little green snake in the new grass glides out of our path. But we pass on; we must reach the hollow in the meadow where strange, shrill voices are piping in a chorus more deafening than the vesper hymn of the million sparrows which congregate on the bare twigs of the trees in the old graveyard of King's Chapel, in Boston, at five in the afternoon.

At last we reach the grassy margin of a shallow pool, only to find—nothing! And somehow we have succeeded in silencing the innumerable voices. Apparently there is nothing to do but to sit down on the end of a neighboring log and patiently wait. Soon a venturesome peeper begins again; then another, and another, until in about ten minutes the chorus is going again full blast. It proceeds from a hundred little throats of frogs less than an inch long, all but invisible in the shallow pool.

Hyla pickeringii—for this is the name of the noisy creature—is a familiar representative of the *Hylidæ* family, and is the earliest piper of spring in the cold bogs and meadows of the hill country. Farther south the rattling note of the cricket frog is heard quite as early, and even that of the common toad. But Pickering's *Hyla* starts in with emphatic

THE MUSKRAT.

FIBER ZIBETHICUS.

"Busily engaged in gnawing
a tender twig."

Photographed from life by
W. Lyman Underwood.

insistence on the fact that spring is here, notwithstanding the patches of meadow snow and ice which
still linger on the shadowy borders. The more
southern pipers do not have to brave these last footprints of the winter king so continually, and I can
not therefore consider them the earliest of all spring
singers.

It is a most remarkable circumstance that Pickering's *Hyla* is always heard, but is seldom seen. He
has a disappointing way of
submerging himself to his
very eyelids in the chilly bog.
With the mercury at fifty degrees he will pipe up at about
four or five in the afternoon. If
we wish to catch him in the act
we must choose a warmer day,
when the mercury stands at sixty
degrees, sit patiently and immova-
bly on the log for a good half hour,
and scan the surface of the pool near the margin with
an opera glass. Here we will be sure to see the bulgy
eyes and the tip of the nose just appearing above
the water, and if we are fortunate, we may see one
of the tiny ocher-yellow creatures perched on some
withered cat-tail leaf, singing his song in plain view
through the glass. Such a tremendous effort he

Spring Peeper
(*Hyla pickeringii*),
" swelling his throat."

makes to throw out the liquid whistle, no wonder it can be heard on a still afternoon nearly a quarter of a mile away! Beneath his chin the skin is swelled out like a brownish-white bubble half the size of his whole body. Imagine a man swelling his throat thus until it took a balloon shape fully three feet in diameter, and then letting the thing collapse with a deafening scream that could be heard fully eighteen miles! Yet this, supposing the *Hyla's* size and voice could be proportionately increased, is exactly what would happen.

The muscular effort which the tiny creature makes to empty his lungs seems not only to collapse the "bubble," but most of the body, so that when he has let out one shrill whistle there is apparently nothing left but his back, head, and legs. But in another instant he has swelled again, and the performance goes on with no evidence that even the smallest blood-vessel will burst. Different individuals answer each other in different tones, but the dominant one is E slurred to F, in the highest octave on the piano, and the song is pitched — by a slight effort of the imagination —in the key of F minor. Other individuals with larger throats disturb this key by singing thus, and still others exasperatingly out of time and tune

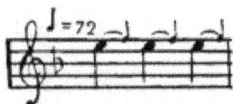

sing either sharp or flat. So the whole effect is shrill rather than melodic, notwithstanding the fact that the F is constantly suggesting the finale of a plaintive melody.

But that is just like Nature—she is ever suggesting, and leaving all beyond to our imagination. A close examination of the body of the little frog emphasizes this fact. There is a strong suggestion of a Saint Andrew's cross on his ocher-colored * back, unmistakably defined in narrow lines, and a narrow dark line extends from the tip of the nose to the eye. The X is quite sufficiently plain to prevent any confusion in the identification of *Hyla pickeringii* with young tree toads (*Hyla versicolor*), or with other frogs of similar size and color, for no other small frog is marked with a cross.

Spring Peeper, showing the St. Andrew's cross on the back.

This *Hyla* is a characteristic tree frog, who with his padded toes ascends the tallest trees with ease, and takes to the water only for a brief time in spring, which is his nuptial season. When the

---

* It may be slightly green, as the frog possesses to a certain degree the power of color change.

breeding season is over, about the first of July,* he
may still be found—but rarely—among the damp,
fallen leaves of the woods, or even in cellars. How
the creatures manage to keep themselves so completely out of sight in spring and summer is always
a mystery. It is not until the latter part of August
that they ascend the trees, and only once in a long
while have I heard the plaintive but unmistakably
clear whistle of one in the woods toward the close of
September. Prof. E. D. Cope speaks of the autumnal voice of this frog thus : " When the wind is casting the first frosted leaves to the ground, a whistle,
weaker than the spring cry, is heard repeated at intervals during the day, from one part of the forest
to another, bearing considerable resemblance to the
note of the purple finch (*Carpodacus purpureus*)
uttered while it is flying."

The geographical distribution of Pickering's *Hyla*
is extensive. He is found from east of the Central
Plains to the Atlantic, and from Canada to Florida
and Texas.

The form of this *Hyla* approaches that of a
more southern genus called *Chorophilus*, one species

* It is a remarkable fact that this *Hyla* is apt to choose temporary pieces of water in the hollows of the meadow for its breeding
places, because, as the season advances and the water evaporates,
whole colonies of its tadpoles dry up and miserably perish in the
hot sun.

PICKERING'S HYLA.

HYLA PICKERINGII.

"In the latter part of August
they ascend the trees."

of which I describe farther on, but it has larger "foot pads."

The cricket frog, or Savannah cricket (*Acris gryllus*), a little creature a trifle over an inch long, commonly found as far north as southern New York, is the only known representative of this genus. In more southern marshes — those, for instance, of New Jersey—we may happen to hear both Pickering's *Hyla* and the cricket frog singing in company.

But *Acris gryllus* has a distinct voice of his own. He does not whistle an uninterrupted note, but breaks into musical crepitations somewhat resembling the broken tone of a rattle whistle. His voice has the same character as that of the common toad, but its quality is more nearly like that of the tree cricket. More than one naturalist has suggested its likeness to the rapid striking together of two

Savannah Cricket
(*Acris gryllus*).

pebbles, but to my ear the pebbles are not musical enough; impart to them some of the cheery jingle of sleighbells and then I will admit the similitude.

In appearance the cricket frog altogether differs

from the *Hyla;* there are no distinct pads on the toes,* and consequently he seldom if ever ascends trees or bushes. His general color is variable. With the tree toad (*Hyla versicolor*) he possesses a certain power of color change, or metachrosis, and while he may be dull green in an environment of green leaves, among dead ones he is quite as likely to be brown. There is a very characteristic blackish, triangular patch between the eyes, the apex of which is directed backward. This is margined by a light color, sometimes greenish, sometimes rusty, and as often dull white. This marginal color of the triangle is continued in a dorsal stripe to the end of the body. The extreme northeasterly limit of this frog is New Haven, Conn.

But there are two varieties of this *Acris,* differing slightly in form and appearance from the species proper; one of northern distribution is called *Acris gryllus crepitans,* and another of southern distribution (from North Carolina to Florida and Louisiana) is called *Acris gryllus gryllus.* With the latter we have nothing to do, as it is south of our range; but the former is likely to engage our attention in the

---

* These are furnished, however, with very slightly enlarged disks.

West as far north as Illinois, and also in the East in southern Pennsylvania.*

William Hamilton Gibson has made a most truthful drawing of the *Acris gryllus crepitans* to accompany his article in Harper's Young People for March 25, 1890. Dr. Abbott also frequently refers to *Acris crepitans*,† but I question whether either he or Mr. Gibson actually heard this species. It is far more likely that they heard the *Acris gryllus;* still, I have no means of positively knowing this. According to Professor Cope, *Acris gryllus crepitans* has *no* record east of Carlisle, Pa.

The subspecies *Acris gryllus crepitans* has three oblique blotches on the sides, which are very prominent, and the limbs are muscular and well developed. ‡

Savannah Cricket
(*Acris gryllus crepitans*).

The note of this species, it is said, may be ex-

---

* More particularly in Carlisle, Cumberland County.

† *Vide* Outings at Odd Times, pages 107, 108; also Days Out of Doors, pages 34–37. I doubt very much though, whether the *Acris* can whistle and crepitate too. This would be contrary to Nature, for reasons which are too many for me to explain.

‡ Professor Cope also gives the following anatomical definition of this subspecies: "*Acris gryllus crepitans.* Hinder foot, not including the tarsus (that part of the foot above the instep), less than half the length of head and body combined; skin tubercles larger; posterior femoral (hind leg) stripe less distinct."

actly imitated by striking two marbles together, first
slowly, then faster and faster, for a succession of
about twenty or thirty beats. The noise can not be
heard at a very great distance.

The little frog is prominently marked on the
back with green, and has the same dark triangle on
the crown as that described for the species proper.
He remains in the tall grass around the marsh, and
seldom if ever ascends a tree or bush. When pur-
sued he leaps extraordinary distances and invariably
makes for the water, into which he disappears just
as we reach the margin after much clumsy slumping
through the bog and vain grabbing at the unattain-
able.   Only one who has lost a frog this
way knows anything about the sudden mental activity of the baffled pursuer as he
stands gazing at the mocking ripples.

The genus *Acris* is distinguished for
its swimming powers. Look at my drawing of the hind leg and note the webbed

Hindleg
(*A. gryllus
crepitans*). toes; now compare this with the hind leg
of *Chorophilus triseriatus* (page 11). and it will be
seen that the latter can not be much of a swimmer.

The *Chorophilus triseriatus*, another singer in
early spring, about the same size as the cricket frog,
may be heard in the West, and in the East as far
north as central New Jersey. This frog is ash-gray

striped with three brown lines, or sometimes fawn color with the brown stripes broader; the yellow-white beneath is distinctly granulated.

Professor Cope says, "It delights in those small and often temporary pieces of water which are inclosed in the densest thickets of spiny *Smilax* and *Rubus*, with scrub oaks, and sur-rounded by the water-loving *Ceph-alanthus*, where no shade interrupts

Three-striped Frog
(*Chorophilus
triseriatus*).

the full glow of sunlight. Here the little frogs may be heard in the hottest part of the day, accompanied by a few *Acris gryllus*, or rarely a *Hyla pickeringii* . . . . As they scarcely swim, when surprised they seek refuge in the edge of the water, with so little movement that their capture is no easy matter."

In southwestern New Jersey the swamps resound with the rattling notes of these frogs throughout the spring and sometimes in the summer. They sing not only in the evening but at midday, just as the common toad does. The music is extremely

Hindleg
(*C. triseri-
atus*).

soft—rising, swelling, and subsiding like the waves of the seashore. I can best represent the song of a single singer thus: The crepitations are not so loud as those of the *Acris*, nor have they the same ringing, sleigh-bell quality. The tone is also of a much lower pitch, and it *very* slightly approaches in quality the bleating tone of the tree toad.

According to Professor Cope, this frog is common in Gloucester County, N. J., and Chester County, Pa.; but since the time in which he wrote (1889) I am inclined to think that the frog has found his way farther to the northeast, and he ought to be heard now in Staten Island and the vicinity. I have certainly heard his voice in the pine barrens not far from Lakewood, N. J.

I can not sufficiently emphasize the fact that every species of living thing has its own particular voice. When once we have heard a single Pickering's *Hyla*, we have heard the characteristic voice of that species, and it is not to be confused for one moment with that of any *other* species. The common frog's droning note can not be mistaken for the rattling note of the *Chorophilus*, or the ringing, jingling note of the *Acris;* nor is the quality * of the note of any one of these species I have named like that of the bubbly-bleaty note of the tree toad.

---

* This, in music, we call "timbre." When I change my tenor voice and sing a falsetto note, and thus imitate the soprano voice, I have altered the *timbre* of the note; although it may still be A, its quality is no longer the same.

I can imitate *Hyla pickeringii* by shrilly whistling E slurred to F in the highest octave on the piano; I need a bass viol to imitate the bullfrog (*Rana catesbiana*); I am sure I do not know how to copy the tree toad's note, unless by making a bleating sound with the lips; I must have a rattle whistle to imitate the *Acris;* and I must hum one note and whistle another to approximate the droning note of the toad. A big chorus of the *Hyla* and *Acris* sounds like jingling sleighbells; a medley of the larger batrachians' voices is like the "tuning up" of a string orchestra.

Quite nearly related to the genus *Chorophilus* is the genus *Hyla,** one species of which (*Hyla pickeringii*) I have already noticed. There are but two other *Hylæ* whose range extends north of North Carolina: one is *Hyla versicolor* (of the same range as *Hyla pickeringii*), and the other is *Hyla ander-*

---

* The genus *Hyla* includes fully one half of the large *Hylidæ* family, which seems to have been created to inhabit the leafy part of the world—especially the tropical part—for the special purpose of holding in check the prolific insect life which might otherwise do an inestimable amount of injury to vegetation. It is the case, therefore, that in those regions where vegetable life abounds there is a proportional increase in the number of species. I question very much whether one could conscientiously kill a toad or a frog who had a full knowledge of the immense number of insects it devoured within a year's time, and the extent of harm that these might have worked on vegetation.

sonii, an extremely rare frog found from New Jersey to Georgia. As only three individuals of this last species had been found up to 1889, we must pass it as an unfamiliar phase of swamp life, and turn our attention to the very common *Hyla versicolor*.

This is the frog familiarly known as the tree toad, which inhabits every hedgerow and tree-girt marsh throughout the country. Professor Verrill records this species as being found at Norway, Me.,

Tree Toad (*Hyla vesicolor*).

which is considered the most easterly point of its range; but at Campton, N. H., scarcely sixty-three miles west of Norway, I have found this frog, if not common, at least so plentiful that I have heard him sing *every* season for the last ten years. It would seem reasonable, then, to move his easterly limit still farther east than Norway. Wherever there are woodlands bordering a marsh or pond, there he will be sure to be heard, at least in June; and I have no doubt but that his voice may be a familiar one in some of the wooded swamps near Portland.

This remarkable tree toad has a compact, squat-

looking figure, the outline of which at all points
might easily touch the circumference of a circle.
The head is broader than it is long. The back of
the creature is generally ashen gray, with strange
blotches of green here and there; but we must not
forget that he can change color, and in an environment of leaves and grass he is decidedly green.
Again, on a lichen-covered log he is quite likely to
be brown-gray, and on the rough trunk of the swamp
maple (*Acer rubrum*) an uncompromising brown.
In fact he possesses the power of metachrosis (color
change) to a wonderful degree; hence his specific
title *versicolor*. This change, however, is not accomplished quickly. His back is covered with warty
excrescences; beneath his body, on the lighter skin,
are distinct granulations; and a characteristic loose
fold extending across the chest indicates that he does
not " fit his clothes."

The eggs of *Hyla versicolor* are laid in small
packets on blades of grass, slender sticks, and the
stems of weeds, in shallow pools. All through the
breeding season, in May or June, the bleating note
of this frog may be heard after the sun goes down,
in different parts of the swamp, one voice respond-
ing to another, or perhaps both mingling. I have
counted about eight notes given out in one second
and a half. This is a fair average utterance of one

individual. Intervals of about four seconds and a
half occur with indifferent regularity. One can not
quite depend on the tree toad for synchronous
effect; it is a sort of go-as-you-please musical con-
versation which he keeps up, very often confused
by two or three speaking at the same time; but the
winning little voices are pleasing and entertaining,
and the "word" that is passed around is reassuring.

There are rarely more than three or four of these
frogs congregated in one spot, and it may often be
quite a distance to the next assembly. The voices
are strung along in the dusk of evening somewhat
thus:

By the time No. 4 begins No. 1 breaks in again,
and we have a duet; then comes No. 2 alone;
then No. 3 accompanied by No. 4; and presently, in
the irregularity of the succession, we have a trio.
Imagine a few tiny lambs bleating thus: "Tur-r-r-r-t,
Tre-t-t-t-t," and the simile is as complete as I can
make it. Later in the season these voices come from
the hedges and the orchards; the frogs have left their
aquatic retreats. A Mr. Geismar, who kept several
in his vivarium, has recorded a remarkable instance
of their domestication. Both window and vivarium

being left open during part of the day the frogs
would leave the house and establish themselves on
the trees in the orchard, where their
voices could be heard throughout the
evening. During the night they would
return to the house, and would appear
in their usual places in the morning.

Hyla versicolor is not only remarkable for his change of color and his
winning voice, but also for his "foot
pads," my drawing of which will show

The
"foot-pads" of
the Tree Toad.

their high development. Not-
ing these strange little
disks on the tips
of the toes, which
closely adhere to
the surface on
which the crea-
ture stands, the
fact will not ap-
pear so surprising
that he can stand near-
ly upside down! It is
perfectly plain, too, by

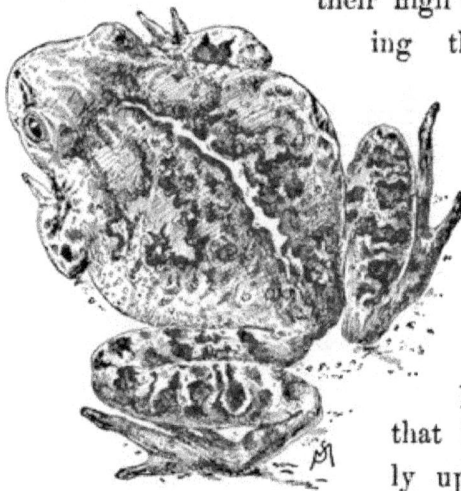

Common Toad.

the webbed feet, that the little acrobat is a fair
swimmer.

Last, but by no means least among the batrachian

3

singers of spring, comes the common toad (*Bufo americanus*). The poor, brown, warty creature which is so repulsive in appearance, and which one shudders to touch, possesses one of the sweetest voices of spring—a dreamy, lulling, musical voice, well fitted to sing the slumber song of Nature, and transport every living thing in woodland and meadow to the mysterious land of dreams. The birds, it is true, may be thus sung to sleep, but not so with all the rest of the animal creation; most of it delights to prowl about all night long, just as Robert Louis Stevenson says, and none of it cares a straw for an accompanying nocturne:

> " The squalling cat and the squeaking mouse,
>   The howling dog by the door of the house,
>   The bat that lies in bed at noon,
>   All love to be out by the light of the moon."

By moonlight the song of the toad seems even more entrancing; but cat and weasel, coon and skunk, fox and bat—all are intent on prey, and our lullaby singers make some of it.

Every dweller in the country is familiar with the voice of *Bufo americanus*. In the breeding season, from April to June, the toad resorts to the swampy parts of the meadow, and there winds his horn for the delectation of his mate. The sound is a some-

what cricketlike but prolonged "Wur-r-r-r-r," which can be closely imitated by humming and softly whistling the following notes together:
In a large congregation of toads the chorus, by no means shrill or noisy, is remarkable for its effect of harmony. Although the note is sustained, it is broken by exceedingly rapid crepitations which it is impossible for the ear to follow. The "locust," which, years ago, boys used to construct from a soda-bottle neck, a piece of kid glove, a woven bit of horsehair, and a stick, produced a very similar but less musical sound. In singing, the toad swells his throat to a whitish, bubblelike form, which collapses when the sound ceases; then after two or three movements of the lips, as though to pucker them for another effort, he swells up again, and continues for the space of about seven seconds more. He repeats this performance an indefinite number of times, and finally, upon a slight and sudden movement of the observer, disappears among the weeds on the border of the pond. So much for his "Liebeslied."

In some secluded part of the pond the female deposits the eggs, which are inclosed in a long, thick-walled tube of transparent albumen, in the water. These tubes lie in long spiral strings on the bottom, and the dark-colored young hatch out quite early.

Finally, after the consummation of the metamorphosis, they appear in a completed form (tinier than that of the *Hylæ* at the same age) along the margin of the water—veritable pygmy toads.

In midsummer the toad takes up his abode under one's doorstep, and issues forth in the early evening to secure his insect food. I have a great admiration for a certain big fellow who frequents my garden during the night season and makes way with an immense number of insects. He is not disturbed by my presence in the cool of the evening when I water the flowers, and hops about in and out among the poppies and nasturtiums with full confidence that his presence there is welcome. I know exactly where his home is (under the front steps) and can tell pretty nearly at what time he will sally out in the gloaming. He is undoubtedly a creature of systematic habits, and possesses but one fault: he strays beyond the garden limits, and establishes himself about 10 P. M. on the plank walk outside. Here he is in constant danger of being stepped upon with others of his kind who will not stay in the grass.

If one has not an unconquerable aversion to toads it is worth while to corner a big fellow and scratch him on the back. If he is scratched on the right side he will lean over that way, just as a cat does whose cheek is rubbed; if scratched on the left side he leans to the left; if scratched on both sides he squats with content, and, I imagine, an expression of satisfaction settles in his fishy eye.

I do not suppose a toad has any parasite to bite his tough, warty back; the frog, though, does unfortunately have a certain low parasitic form of life which inhabits his blood.* About every creature in the world, however, is likely to furnish another smaller world for yet smaller creatures to live in, and the frog is no exception to the rule. There is more truth than nonsense in the suggestive doggerel that runs:

" Little fleas have lesser fleas upon their backs to bite 'em,
    And these fleas have lesser fleas, *ad infinitum.*
    Great fleas have greater fleas upon their backs to go on,
    And these fleas have greater fleas and greater fleas, and
        so on!"

---

* There have been certain sausagelike parasites discovered in the blood of *Rana esculenta.* Dr. Gaule found in this frog's red blood-corpuscles, mobile corpuscles, elongate, and pointed at the extremities. These issued from the cells, which they could drag after them for some time, but after a while became motionless, and finally died and disappeared.

CHAPTER II.

THE CROAKERS.

Familiar Members of the Tribe Rana.

WE have already considered the soloists of the batrachian orchestra, and now the musicians who represent the 'cello and the bass viol must engage our notice. A hundred croaking voices reach our ears from the vicinity of the frog pond, and many of them possess a distinct individuality. The "croaks" are not all alike: there is the basso profundo of the bullfrog, the barytone of the green frog, and several other strange tones of still stranger batrachians, all of which are easily distinguished apart.

The genus *Rana*,* to which these croakers belong, is an extensive division of the large family *Ranidæ*. It includes no less than one hundred and

---

* The frogs belonging to the genus *Rana* are well protected from their enemies by an extremely acrid secretion of the skin. Cats and dogs avoid them as a rule, not, however, without exceptions; but snakes appear to differ in their tastes, and the great number of frogs they swallow in the springtime is beyond calculation.—*Cope.*

eight species, according to Mr. Boulanger, but of these only six are common enough in our northeastern States to attract our notice. These are:

1. *Rana virescens virescens*, the leopard frog; a subspecies of *Rana virescens* (*Rana halecina*, of other authors), a bright-green frog found along our seacoast and the adjacent country.

2. *Rana palustris*, a light-brown frog found in cold springs and streamlets.

3. *Rana septentrionalis*, a round-spotted frog found in northern New York and the northwest.

4. *Rana clamata*, the green frog, common everywhere.

5. *Rana catesbiana*, the bullfrog, the largest species of all, also common.

6. *Rana sylvatica*, the wood frog, common everywhere in our woodlands.

The prettiest fellow of them all is the leopard frog, *Rana virescens virescens*, about two and a half inches long. A bright copper-colored line begins at his nose and ends at his eye; a second line of yellowish white reaches

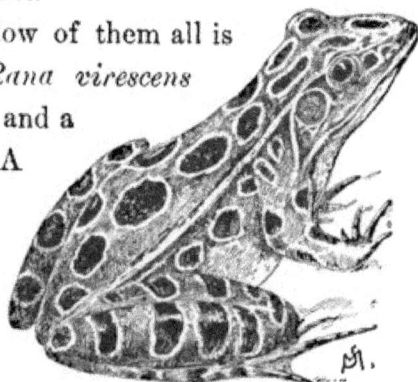

Leopard Frog
(*Rana virescens virescens*).

from the nose to the shoulder. The eyes are large
and prominent, the nose is pointed, and the general
color of the body above is yellowish green marked
with oval *spots of olive* margined with *bright yellow*.
These spots are arranged in two rows on the back,
and in two others less distinct on the sides. Under-
neath, the body is silver-white at the mouth and yellow-white at the abdomen. There is a characteristic
longitudinal band on the front of the thigh.

This species is found in great numbers in the
swamps that border the creeks and rivers of the Atlantic coast; but inland, except in the Mississippi
Valley, it is rather rare. According to Professor
Cope, with the *Acris gryllus* it is the first species
heard in spring, and although a single voice is not
loud, the noise produced by thousands of them close
at hand is deafening, and can be heard many miles
away. This frog "*clucks*" almost exactly like a hen,
and in about the same key;
but the noise of a large
number sounds more like a
number of ducks quacking, but not without a decidedly musical ring. I can not, of course, indicate
what difference there may be between the voices of
the species proper (*Rana virescens* or *Rana halecina*)
and this subspecies, but I am inclined to believe that
there is none.

Rana palustris is a frog of the same size as *Rana virescens virescens,* but of entirely different color and tune. His voice is hoarse, and his note is a long, low croak, resembling, as Professor Cope says, the tearing of some coarse material; I should suggest burlap, and add that the tone is anywhere from F to A below middle C on the piano.

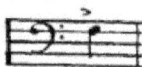

This frog lives around cold streams and springs, and is very commonly seen in the grass. In habit he is not gregarious like *Rana virescens virescens,* but on the contrary is rather solitary. He is the most abundant frog in the Alleghany Mountains, but is common throughout all the States east of the Mississippi River. In agility he is only excelled by the wood frog (*Rana sylvatica*),

Brown Frog
(*Rana palustris*).

which he slightly resembles in point of *color,* lacking, however, the dash of black behind the eye. With one long, graceful leap this athletic batrachian covers the ground with the ease of a deer, and leaves his pursuer far in the rear. He has rather a disagreeable odor.

The nose of this species is more obtuse than that of *Rana virescens virescens*, and the general color of the back is light brown, well covered with *oblong spots of dark brown* regularly arranged on either side. Between these spots and another similar series lower down on the side is a bright yellow line. The *wood* frog's color is generally tan brown, but he is without conspicuous spots.

The northern frog (*Rana septentrionalis*), which is the least familiar one of my group, is distinguished for its disagreeable odor. It has a somewhat broad, stout body, a narrow head, and a rough but not tuberculated skin. The color above is light olive, covered on the lower half of the back with *large, nearly circular blotches of brown.* The legs have a few blotches, but no bands. Beneath, the color is a uniform dull whitish yellow. Compared with *Rana clamata*,* the species next described, this

Northern Frog
(*Rana septentrionalis*).

---

* *Vide* Batrachia of North America. E. D. Cope.

frog has a browner color, larger eyes, longer fingers, and longer but less webbed feet. According to Professor Cope, the variations of *Rana septentrionalis* are greater than those of any other North American species of this genus.

The northern frog is about two inches long in maturity, and is found only in the north country from Garrison's Creek, near Sackett's Harbor (Lake Ontario), N. Y., northward to Canada, and westward to Minnesota.

Dr. J. H. Garnier, who has given a detailed account of the habits of this species as observed by him at Lucknow, Ontario, says it possesses the odor of the mink, and is particularly offensive on being handled. It is a thoroughly aquatic species, which seeks its food— insects and small fishes — in the water only. I know nothing of its voice.

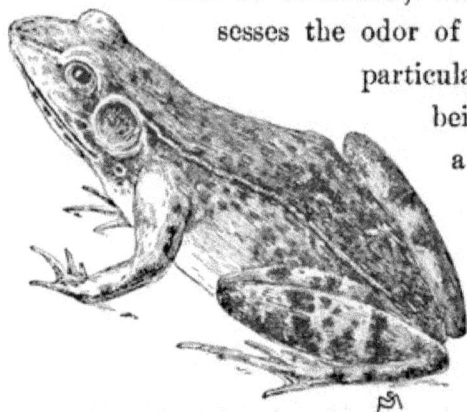

Green Frog (*Rana clamata*).

The green frog (*Rana clamata*)—or the noisy frog, as his Latin specific title would seem to suggest (a very common batrachian, about three inches

long)—is the one whose familiar nasal "gum-m-m"
or "chun-n-ng" is heard in every pool and frog pond
from one end of the country to the other.   He generally waits on the margin until we approach within
a yard of his retreat, and then slumps into the pool
with a short and derisive "g-m-m" in C, one octave
below middle C on the piano, thus:
Often the note will be as high as E;
but in any event it is not a noisy voice which one
hears, and the Latin name seems entirely misapplied,
more particularly as these frogs do not congregate in
large and clamorous assemblies like *Hyla pickeringii*
or *Rana virescens virescens*.   On the contrary, *Rana
clamata* lives alone or with one or more companions.
We will frequently see him seated on a lily pad or
on the shaded margin of the pond, where he occasionally makes a gulping answer to a fellow frog over
on the other side.

In form *Rana clamata* is rather stout, with a
head longer than it is broad, and very large ear
drums.   The hind feet are strongly webbed, and the
skin of the back is more or less rough.   In color the
frog is decidedly green, the upper parts quite bright
and the lower parts deepening to a dull olive hue.
Beneath, the coloring is dull white merging into yellow under the chin; the hind legs are marked with
three or four transverse dark bands.

The next nearest relative of *Rana clamata* is the bullfrog (*Rana catesbiana*), the largest of all the American species; he frequently measures four and a half inches from the nose to the end of the body.

He is the bass viol of the batrachian orchestra, and the king of all the croaking tribe of *Rana*, but also a sort of cannibal into the bargain, for he is known to feast on his own tadpole progeny. But this is a bad habit not wholly confined to the big *Rana catesbiana*. Any one who has fished for frogs with a bit of red worsted tied to a fishhook knows how the gaping, wide-mouthed creatures will snap at anything that comes along without discrimination; in fact, a tadpole for bait will do almost as well as a bit of red worsted. *Apropos* of this fact, Dr. Abbott's remarks about the voracity of frogs are well worth repeating:

The Bullfrog (*Rana catesbiana*).

"While feeding an Anderson's *Hyla* with flies a

few days ago, which it takes from my fingers, I was
startled by the on-rush of a little wood frog, which,
impatient for its own dinner, seriously attempted to
swallow both the tree toad and my fingers at one
mighty gulp. . . . With widely gaping jaws, which
were distended before the leap was made, the frog attempted to scoop up the toad and swallow it, or get
such a hold as would make subsequent swallowing
an easy task; and yet the difference in size of the
two creatures was very little. As for the tree toad,
it took the whole proceeding as a matter of course,
not moving a muscle even when such great danger
was apparently imminent. The whole tribe of tail-
less batrachians is much alike in this respect, seemingly taking it for granted that they were born to be
eaten, and stuff themselves until fate wills it that
they go to stuff others. . . . I have seen little fellows
just from the tadpole state in dangerous proximity
to patriarchal bullfrogs, which were then only waiting for their appetites to return to swallow a half
dozen of their own grandchildren!"

Rana catesbiana is much less green than *Rana
clamata;* the color of the back is dull olive, sometimes marked with darker blotches or bands, the
positions of which are not always the same. The
head is usually yellowish olive-green, and the lower
part of the body much darker. Beneath, the crea-

THE BULLFROG.

RANA CATESBIANA.

" Tuneful scrapings on a
moonlight night."

ture is yellowish white, much deeper in tone under the chin.   In different localities the frog is differently marked, and it is therefore impossible to define any standard of *color* whereby the species may be identified. The head is as broad as it is long, and the hind feet are *widely webbed*. A characteristic mark of this species is the fold in the skin, which begins behind the eye, curves over the dark round spot which is really the ear, and descends to a point below the lower jaw, losing itself in the yellow skin under the arm on the breast. This is the only fold of skin on the frog, and it is inconspicuous beyond the ear; but a sharp eye may easily detect its course beyond that point.

Every one knows the bullfrog's note; and that his hoarse voice in the distance, so nearly resembling the roar of a bull, should have occasioned his name, goes without saying. Still, as I have remarked before, there is a musical tone to nearly every sound in Nature's world, and our bullfrog is not an exception to the rule. He is the double bass of the midsummer orchestra, and no stretch of the imagination is required to hear his tuneful scrapings on a moonlight night ranging through the following chords:

Rum jugo'rum: jugo' rum: more rum-o'rum more rum o'rum.

There are often as many discords as there are harmonies, I will admit ; but there, again, is Nature's suggestiveness. She simply suggests the harmony, and we assimilate it ; a little imagination does the rest, and "jug o' rum, jug o' rum, more rum, more rum" is quite a justifiable simile, although it reflects on the character of the woodsman more than it does on that of the batrachian. There is a humorous fitting of tones to syllables often scraped on the bass viol during an intermission of the string orchestra, running thus : Hum those tones to a musician and his response is a smile of recognition ; they

What'll you have to drink?

suggest but one idea to the German mind—beer. I am inclined to think the American woodsman is responsible for the suggestive syllables connected with the bullfrog's sonorous croak.

The bullfrog prefers the larger bodies of water, especially where these are surrounded by evergreen forests, and he haunts the shores where thickets and underbrush make his home inaccessible. The voice is not heard until the arrival of warm weather, and it continues through every evening during the summer ; it may occasionally be heard for a distance of two miles.

Dr. Garnier points out certain similar characteristics of the three species, *Rana septentrio-*

nalis, Rana clamata, and *Rana catesbiana,* which I copy :

1. They have no *chant d'amour* in spring.

2. They retire early to hibernate with the first autumnal frost.

3. They live in the water and lie in wait for their food, never hunting for it on land.

4. They poise the body on floating weeds, or sit on the bank, or on any bit of stick or log that suits their purpose.

5. Their tadpoles require two years in which to mature.

6. Their notes are produced by inflating the throat pouch and suddenly expelling the air; whereas in *Rana virescens,* etc., there is a pouch on either side near the angle of the jaws.

7. They are all tinged with yellowish green under the chin.

The wood frog (*Rana sylvatica*) is a distinctly sylvan

Wood Frog (*Rana sylvatica*).

character, he is frequently found among the dead and moist leaves on the border of the brook which

4

finds its way among the ferny hollows of the hillside forest. This frog is susceptible to the color of his surroundings, and changes from the tan color of a dead leaf to the *green* of a living one with considerable ease. In general his color is tan brown, and his characteristic mark is a blackish patch extending from behind the eye to a point just over the shoulder. Often his back will be strong buffish gray, with a tinging of brown on either side. There are three or four transverse dark bands across the thighs, and a few scattered black spots will be found on the sides.

The nose of this species is rather pointed, and the limbs are long and slender, with the hind feet well webbed. The frog is therefore a good swimmer; but as a leaper he holds the record. When one spies a dull brown, slender-legged frog among the leaves around a woodland spring, or even in the recesses of the forest where there is no water near, and this frog takes a flying leap, disappearing entirely—perhaps landing somewhere in the next county—one may be pretty sure that it is none other than *Rana sylvatica*.

In early April we may hear the spasmodic and hoarse croak of the wood frog near the pond, to which he resorts in the short breeding season; but in the summer he takes to the woods again, and remains there for the rest of the year. His voice is pitched about an octave below middle C, and it is really not often heard after May; in fact, this frog is the most silent one of the genus *Rana*.

CHAPTER III.

The Salamanders.

AFTER leaving the clamorous frogs, one experiences a sense of relief in coming to the voiceless salamander—lizard as he is wrongly called. Now the lizard and the salamander belong to two separate families of widely different character. The lizard is covered with imbricated or granular scales; he is the small relation of the alligator. The salamander is smooth-skinned; he is the elongated relation of the frog. The lizard is a *saurian reptile*, the principal characteristics of which are the scales, the claws to the toes, the undilated mouth, the toothed jaws, and the eggs with a hard shell or skin, the young from which do *not* undergo a metamorphosis. The salamander is a *batrachian*, with a skin as smooth as a catfish, toes without claws, dilated mouth, and young which are metamorphosed.

The salamander was credited with the most remarkable attributes in days of old. His bite was

36

considered fatal, and anything which his saliva touched was said to become poisonous. But the principal absurdity connected with this generally aquatic creature was that he could resist fire—in fact, could extinguish it. Bacon says: "There is an ancient received tradition of the salamander that it liveth in fire, and hath force also to extinguish the fire." And Shakespeare makes Falstaff say: "I have maintained that salamander of yours with fire any time this two and thirty years; God reward me for it!" Even in colonial times a superstitious connection of salamanders with the fire on the kitchen hearth was rife in the minds of simple folk, and old dying embers were said to breed them.

But between fire and water the salamander chooses the latter; and although some of the species are terrestrial in habit, many of them are decidedly aquatic —our little red salamander, for instance. Most of the "lizards," however, are found under the stones on the margin of the brook or the ditch; but not a few hide among the damp, withered leaves of the forest floor.

One of the common batrachians of the West is named *Necturus maculatus*—the spotted *Necturus*. His back is crowded with whitish specks, which reduce the general brown color to a pattern in fine lines. Along the back are also arranged superior rows of dark brown spots. The branchial (gilled) formations of this strange creature are very conspicuous, the head and muzzle are flat, the body is proportionally short, and there are but four toes to each foot.

Spotted Necturus (*Necturus maculatus*).

He is entirely aquatic.

That still stranger-looking creature, common on the bottoms of rivers in Ohio, called the hellbender (*Cryptobranchus allegheniensis,* Cope *),

The Hellbender
(*Cryptobranchus allegheniensis*).

is horrible in name only, but yet far from being agreeable in appearance. He is a reptile, every inch. The head is flat and broad, the tail is half as long as the head and body together, the mouth is wide, and the legs are short, with an extensive fold of skin

* Also called *Protonopsis horridus.*

between the armpit and the extremity of the outer
" finger."

This harmless reptile is a pale leaden color with
indistinct brown spots on the back. Both this and
the preceding species have a more eellike than lizardlike appearance. They are about a foot long.

The hellbender is distributed from western New
York to Georgia and Louisiana, and westward to
Iowa. He is entirely aquatic in his habits, and is
frequently " hooked " by fishermen on the
Ohio River.

A more lizardlike and attractive creature than the hellbender is the salamander named *Amblystoma punctatum*, distinguished for a smooth
skin pitted
with pores
which are
most numerous
about the tail,

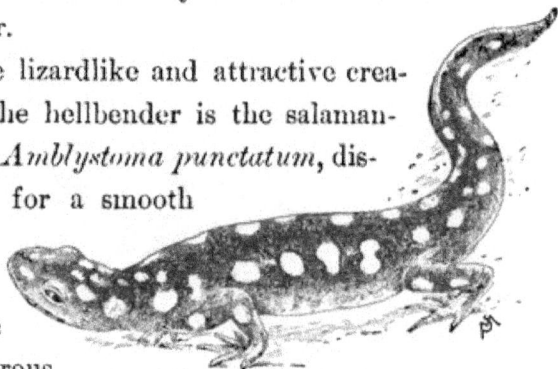

Violet Salamander (*Amblystoma punctatum*).

and for the milky juice which exudes from the darker
colored portions of it. The general color of this salamander is leaden black, and on each side of the back
are a series of circular, or nearly circular, regularly
arranged yellow spots about as large as the eye. On
the sides, and beneath, are some scattered specks
of bluish white on a lighter leaden-colored ground,

which impart a somewhat plum-colored hue to the
creature.

The eggs of this species are surrounded by large
masses of albuminous matter, which are deposited in
pools, ditches, and streamlets.   Upon a closer examination these masses will be found to consist of a number of hollow spheres about a quarter of an inch in
diameter, connected together by a transparent jelly.
Within each sphere is the embryo of a young salamander.   In due season the half-developed, fishlike
creature, freed from the gelatinous envelope, com-
pletes its growth in the quiet water, and finally de-
velops four legs, which sprout from the body and ter-
minate first with three,   then four, and
finally five toes.   This salamander is common
from New York
westward and south-
ward.   The length
of an average specimen at
maturity is about six inches.

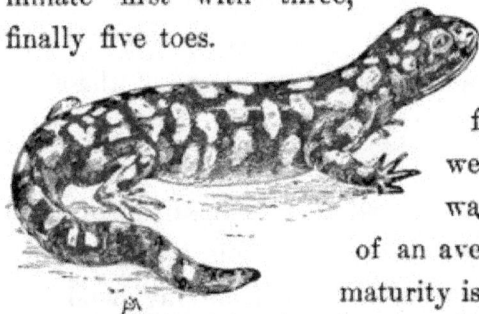

Tiger-spotted Salamander
(*Amblystoma tigrinum*).

Another closely allied
species is the *Amblystoma*
tigrinum, sometimes ten inches in length, but generally not more than seven.   The color of this species
is leaden black of a brownish tone; on the upper
parts, generally on the sides of the tail and limbs, are

sharply defined yellow spots about the size of the eye, less symmetrically arranged than those of *Amblystoma punctatum ;* beneath, the dull white color is sometimes, but not always, blotched with yellow. The head is proportionally small, the body thick and wide, and the legs stout and short.

The young of this species are said to be very abundant in all still water in the far West. They are exceedingly voracious and bite at the hook readily. Late in the summer they complete their metamorphoses and take to the land, where they hide in the holes of woodchucks, badgers, etc. Professor Cope describes a captive salamander of this species (it came from New Jersey) which occupied a burrow in the soil of his fernery for several weeks. The burrow had two openings, and from one of these the head of the creature could usually be seen, with the little eyes intently watching what was going on in the outer world. I had two such salamanders in captivity in my own fernery for about a year. They became perfectly tame, and ate from my hand. It was amusing to watch the little heads deliberately turn for a better view of some interesting object.

Amblystoma tigrinum is common from southern New York southward and westward, and is especially abundant near Beasley's Point, between Cape May and Atlantic City, N. J. A specimen is even re-

corded from Ottawa, so it is apparent that its geographical distribution is very wide.

The most elongated and slender native species
of salamander is the *Plethodon cinereus*, whose body
and tail, cylindrical throughout, meas-
ure about four inches in

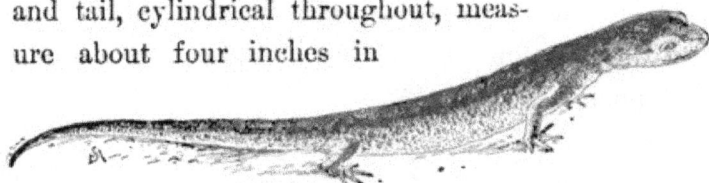

Plethodon cinereus.

length; the tail is sometimes considerably longer than
the head and body. The color above is dark brown,
and below it is dull white, so thickly sprinkled with
mottled brown that the general appearance is like
that of "pepper and salt."

This little fellow is characteristically sylvan. His
habits are exclusively terrestrial; he is never found
(even in the larval stage) in the water. He hides
under the stones and fallen trunks in the forests
everywhere, and never strays to the open fields. The
eggs are laid in a little package beneath a stone
in a damp place; when the young emerge they are
provided with branchiæ (gills of a fringelike appearance), but these soon vanish, and very small specimens are often found without them. I do not recollect that I have ever found this salamander in New
England; but in the woodlands of southern New

York he is far from uncommon. That, however, is a matter of personal experience. Professor Cope says that this species, found throughout the United States east of the Mississippi River, is apparently more abundant in the Middle States than elsewhere, and that its northern range is central Maine, Ontario, and Michigan.

A very common variety of this species is the red-backed salamander (*Plethodon cinereus erythronotus*). There is prac- tically no difference be- tween the proportions and characteristics of this sub-species and those of *Plethodon* *cinereus*. In *ap- pearance* there is a difference; the back of *Plethodon cinereus erythronotus* is marked with a broad red stripe

Red-backed Salamander
(*P. cinereus erythronotus*).

which begins at the neck and finishes at the tip of the tail. There is a mottled appearance at the middle of the stripe which does not affect this color. The stripe is also variable in tone; sometimes it is brick-red, occasionally it is pinkish, and at other times it is pale orange.*

---

* When it is this color we are liable to confuse it with the species *Desmognathus ochrophæa*, but the body of the latter is stouter, and its under parts are never yellow.

This species is common on the west side of Lake Champlain, in Essex County, N. Y., in southern New England, in the southern Catskills (at Pine Hill), and in New Jersey, at least according to my experience and that of several others. Its distribution, however, is quite parallel with that of *Plethodon cinereus*. At his home in New Jersey, Dr. Abbott once shook one from a stick of wood which he was about to place on the fire, and the creature, instead of supporting its reputation of being a "fire-eater," scampered away from the hearth in frantic alarm.

Another species closely allied to the above, but stouter in figure, called *Plethodon glutinosus*, the

Plethodon glutinosus.

sticky salamander, has a wide range from Maine to Texas. Professor Cope says he found it more abundant in Pennsylvania and New York than in southwestern Virginia. It is also said to be common in Massachusetts and Maine.* The skin of this salamander is everywhere lined with little glands which

---

* *Vide* Batrachia of North America. Cope.

secrete a milky juice; these glands are largest on the upper surface of the tail, and more scattered on the under parts.

The head of the sticky salamander is broad, the eyes are large and prominent, and the toes are slightly swollen at the ends. The color of the back is leaden black, and on the sides are tiny silvery gray specks. The back is sometimes entirely without spots, or they are exceedingly minute. This salamander is also terrestrial in his habits. He is found most commonly in the mountainous districts of the North and South, and his favorite haunts are the crevices of rocky ledges and the hollows in decaying logs. His total length is a little less than six inches.

This species is distinguished from *Plethodon cinereus* by its broader figure, larger limbs, less webbed toes, and silvery side spots.

The next salamanders which should engage our attention belong to the genus *Spelerpes*, which is re-

Two-striped yellow Salamander (*Spelerpes bilineatus*).

markable for its bright colors, usually red or yellow. The two-striped salamander (*Spelerpes bilineatus*) is yellow, with a slightly brownish tinge on the back, and

two dark brown lines, one on either side. The under
parts are a spotless citron yellow. The pretty little
creature is scarcely more than three inches in length ;
his tiny legs are terminated by the slenderest of toes,
and his small figure is altogether dainty and attractive.
Very probably he is the salamander to which Dr.
Abbott refers in Days Out of Doors, thus : " Deeper
in the drifted mass, where the trickling waters of a
little spring had formed a shallow pool, were numbers
of long, lithe yellow salamanders, which I had not
found before, and so had held were not to be included
in our fauna. I forgot for the time that others might
have been more fortunate, as was the case." Yes,
these amber-yellow salamanders, even if they are not
common in New Jersey, are somewhat common in
New York—in the southern Catskills, for instance—
and in Pennsylvania. The northern range of the
species is extended with decreasing numbers to the
borders of Maine, and, although specimens may not
be common, perhaps, in New Hampshire, I have found
one as far north as Squam Lake. Southwardly and
westwardly this species is found in Florida and Ohio.
The yellow salamander is aquatic to a certain extent,
and frequents shallow brooks, stony swamps, and cold
springs ; but I have also found the little fellow
among the weeds that border the brook. He is a
sprightly creature, and wriggles away from the hand

THE HOME OF THE RED
SALAMANDER.

SPELERPES RUBRA.

THE MCCANN BROOK,
CAMPTON, N. H.

which captures him with the slightest opportunity that is offered.

A far commoner type of *Spelerpes* is the red salamander (*Spelerpes rubra*), which is found in almost every mountain tarn or brook in the north country. This is the familiar, so-called "red lizard," perhaps five inches long at most, whose brilliant coloring in the green setting of the hillside spring is an unexpected and delightful surprise to one who gazes upon it for the first time. In habits this creature is decidedly aquatic, as he never goes beyond the precincts

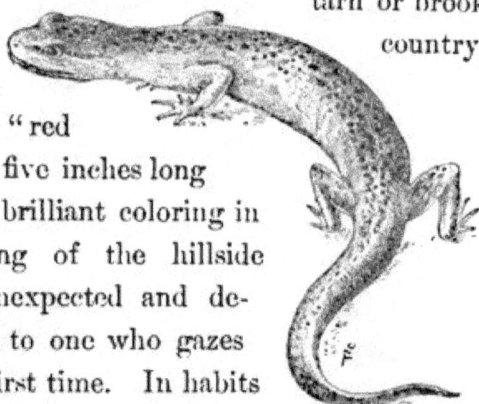

Red Salamander
(*Spelerpes rubra*).

of the brook except in rainy weather. On a very rainy day last summer one made his appearance on the back-door step of my cottage in the White Mountains, evidently after straying from the spring a hundred feet behind the house ; but wet days are the only ones for salamanders to travel in. There is no fear of "drying up" *en route*, and the wide world, however wet, is more interesting than the stony environment of the brook ; so I captured the adventurous salamander and gave him a view of life in my studio from the confines of a fish globe.

But he proved very uninteresting. He did not favor me with his mysterious song, which I had read so much about, and he ate nothing that was set before him. In fact, his existence proved to be a very monotonous one from my point of view, so I gave him his liberty.

He came on a rainy day, and I let him go on another. There is nothing like being consistent. It is well not to forget that it occasionally rains frogs and salamanders, according to the dictum of some simple-minded people, and it is wisest to choose a wet day, and thus not shake the faith of a believer! But there is a very strange thing connected with the little · red salamander, which is the more remarkable because there seems to be but one record of it. I refer to the *voice* ascribed to the creature. It seems very doubtful whether he *has* any voice.* Possibly I am the most unreasonable of skeptics in this matter, but I have a lingering idea that the salamander† which John

---

* I have referred the matter to Professor Garman, of Cambridge, and he is also very skeptical about the salamander's voice. As Professor Garman is one of our leading authorities on batrachians, and as he has never heard a salamander sing, I am inclined to accept his opinion as final.

† " For years I have been trying to ascertain for a certainty the author of that fine plaintive peeping to be heard more or less frequently, according to the weather, in our summer and autumn woods. It is a note that much resembles that of our small marsh frog in spring—the *Hyla*. It is not quite so clear and assured,

Burroughs heard was a scamp and a base deceiver.
He must have been swelling his throat "for the fun
of it," while some Pickering's *Hyla* was piping near
by; but Burroughs not only says he saw and heard
this particular salamander sing, but adds that "it
makes more music in the woods in autumn than any
bird."

Now, in all the time I have known the red salamander—from boyhood—I have never heard him
make any kind of noise. Still, this proves nothing.
He may sing, and all these years I may have missed
the song; but on Staten Island, in Putnam County,
in the Adirondacks, in the Catskills, and in New
England, I have frequently seen him early and late

---

but otherwise much the same. On a very warm October day I
have heard the woods vocal with it; it seemed to proceed from
every stump and tree about one. Ordinarily it is heard only at
intervals throughout the woods. Approach never so cautiously
the spot from which the sound proceeds and it instantly ceases.
. . . 'Is it a frog,' I said, 'the small tree frog. the piper of the
marshes, repeating his spring note?' . . . Doubtless it is, yet I
must see him in the very act. . . . I heard the sound proceed
from beneath the leaves at my feet. Keeping entirely quiet, the
little musician presently emerged, and, lifting himself up on a
small stick, his throat palpitated, and the plaintive note again
came forth. . . . No, it was no frog or toad at all, but the small
red salamander, commonly called lizard. This was the mysterious piper, then, heard from May till November through all our
woods, sometimes on trees, but usually on or near the ground. It
makes more music in the woods in autumn than any bird."—*Pe-
pacton, Chapter V, John Burroughs.*

in the year, yet never have heard him sing. Still, this again proves nothing; there are other places and times that he might have sung, and not every one could be the fortunate listener. But let me draw together some facts which have a favorable bearing on the salamander's voice, and then leave the reader free to form his own opinion.

Professor Cope says of a Western batrachian, *Amphiuma means,* that it resembles the species of *Desmognathus* in the possession of a chirrup or whistle (!). Then he continues, "I do not know of another American salamander which possesses a voice." Also, in an addenda to the work from which I quote,* he says: "Dr. Charles C. Abbott informs me that *Spelerpes rubra* has a distinct whistlelike voice, and states that John Burroughs has also heard it."

Dr. Abbott says, in Outings at Odd Times: "It was only after a hard chase that I captured it" [a red salamander], "and, holding it in my hand until rested, I endeavored to induce it to squeak, for *it is one of the very few that has a voice;* but it was not to be coaxed. It suffered many indignities in silence, and so shamed me by its patience that I gently placed it in the brook."

---

* The Batrachia of North America.

William Hamilton Gibson, in an article entitled Autumn Whistlers, published in Harper's Young People,* also quotes from John Burroughs the same account of the red salamander's voice which I have given in the accompanying footnote; but he does not cite any instance where he heard the voice and saw the singer *himself*.

In a letter contributed to Nature I find Professor Eimer relates his experience connected with a lizard's voice. He remarks that one which he observed on the rocks of Capri had a peculiar voice which is ascribed among reptiles to geckoes and chameleons alone. This lizard, he says, made a peculiarly soft piping sound on being captured, and uttered repeatedly, in quick succession, a series of very sharp tones sounding like " Bschi," and reminding one of the hoarse piping of a mouse or young bird. I suppose this lizard must have been one of the same species which I saw when wandering through the deserted streets of the ancient city of Pompeii. There seemed to be a lizard partly hidden in every nook and cranny of the walls on either hand. Once in a while one scampered with lifted tail across the rough pavement out of my way. Upon capturing two or three, I found they resented handling by squirming about and giv-

* Also published in a volume entitled Sharp Eyes.

ing a vicious nip at one's fingers, but they never
squeaked.

Now this evidence, such as it is, proves but one
thing : that a certain lizard and a salamander or two
do have voices; but these, it seems, are rarely heard.
We have no testimony regarding the voice of *Spelerpes rubra* except that given by Burroughs. The
very fact that he mentions the strange voices as commonly occurring *in the woods from May until November*, suggests the possibility that he may have
heard the *Hyla*, who *do* sing scatteringly in the woods
during this season. Moreover, the fact remains that
Spelerpes rubra is distinctively aquatic. He has no
business to be plaintively "peeping" on trees or on
the ground, especially when it is *not* a rainy day.
Indeed, if we should care to look for a red salamander on *a fine day* we would better go to the spring or
brook at once. He is, as I have intimated, an attractive little creature whose quiet habits are worth
study. In appearance he is far from positive red.
His color is rather a translucent dull orange red, and
sometimes he matches a brick quite perfectly. Along
his back are blackish specks which are more or less
conspicuous in different individuals. In immature
specimens these are not distinct, and in some they are
scarcely perceptible.

The red salamander is generally found beneath a

stone in a cold spring, or oftener in a hollow beside
the stone. He swims with considerable activity, and
is not easily caught as he glides through the water
with limbs pressed against the body and tail undulat-
ing rapidly; but once on land he is at the mercy of
his pursuer. His efforts at locomotion are neither
graceful nor rapid. The food of this species consists of insects.

Still another even more common salamander, perhaps the most abundant one in North America, is
found in the hillside spring. This is *Desmognathus
fusca*, a little mud-colored character scarcely
more than four inches long, which
burrows under the pebbles and
stones, and whose dark
brown color ad-

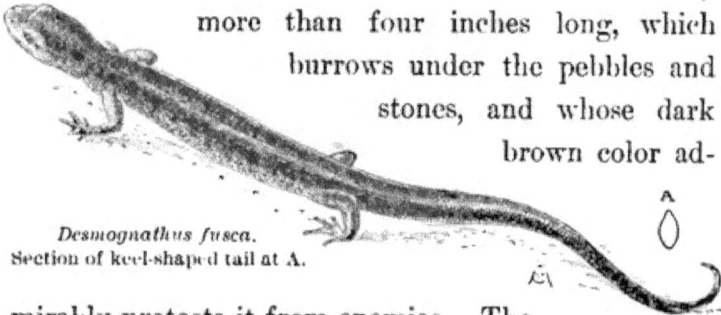

Desmognathus fusca.
Section of keel-shaped tail at A.

mirably protects it from enemies. The
tail of this species is characterized by finlike and
keellike extensions which narrow toward the tip.
Among the wet blackish roots and stones of the
brook the little creature is not easily distinguished
from his surroundings, consequently he escapes our
notice; but turn over a half-dozen stones on the
border of some shallow pool, and the agile move-

ments of one or two wriggling so-called lizards will betray their presence.

I have found this salamander quite plentiful in the shallow brooks of Campton, N. H., particularly where these run through stony, boggy places characterized by blackish mud, and perhaps shaded by the feathery boughs of the hemlock. But the species is common throughout the country, although its eastern limit is probably Essex County, Mass.

The ocher-colored salamander, *Desmognathus ochrophæa*, is an allied species of more local interest, which is found in Essex County, N. Y., and in the Alleghany Mountains. It is abundant in the Black Mountains of North Carolina and northern Pennsylvania. Its color is brownish yellow above, with a dorsal row of spots in darker yellowish color, and on either side of it, lower down, a band of the same color which extends to the tip of the tail. Beneath, it is without spots.

This small species, not more than three inches long, and rarely exceeding half the size of *Desmognathus fusca*, resembles the red-backed salamander, but its figure is stouter. Its tail is rounded, in which respect it differs from *Desmognathus fusca*, and it also differs from the other species of the genus *Desmognathus* in its thoroughly *terrestrial* habits. Instead of hiding under the stones of the brook, it frequents the damp places of the woods where decaying leaves and tree trunks are plenty, particularly those of the hemlock. Professor Cope says he never saw one in the water of streams and river banks.

Desmognathus nigra, another allied species, is a black salamander about six and a half inches long, which is found in the Alleghany Mountains from Pennsylvania southward. It is particularly common in Virginia. This creature is aquatic, and, like *Desmognathus fusca*, inhabits only shallow stony brooks and cold springs in the remote parts of the mountains which afford cool and shady retreats.

I am wholly unable to account for the paragraph which I have quoted on a previous page from Cope's Batrachia of North America. The professor makes no further remark about the *Desmognathus* possessing a whistle. I certainly know *two* of the species of this genus well, but I am not aware that either possesses a voice. Years ago I used to spend hours hunting through the brooks of New Jersey and New Hampshire for salamanders, and these I carried to my home in the city by the dozen—that was my boyish pleasure; but *never* have I heard one whistle. The creatures were apparently voiceless. It seems as though after twenty years of acquaintance with them I ought to have heard one sing; but I have not, and I shall leave it now for my readers to dis-

cover that rare and mysterious music of the so-called
"lizard," which, when it is heard, will prove beyond
a shadow of doubt that these batrachians are *not*
songless.

CHAPTER IV.

OUR ANCIENT ENEMY THE OPHIDIAN.*
Snakes.

A REPTILE † in the fullest sense of the term, the snake glides through the grass and across the road, the most unfortunate and repellent representative of his class. I think Ruskin hit upon the true reason of our aversion to snakes when he said that the creature glided "a bit one way, a bit another, and some of him not at all." That is the one characteristic of the snake—his circumventive motion—which we most dislike; regardless of his reptilian looks, it is sufficient to know that he skims over the ground in so sinuous a way that we can not keep an eye on him. Any attempt to trace his course meets with failure, and before one realizes it, one is stupidly staring at the spot where the creature *was!* We do not like to be tricked this way; such an insidious method of locomotion is a species of deceit indicative of the treacherous character of the beast, so we count him

---

* From ὀφίδιον, a serpent.　† From the Latin *repo*, to crawl.

an evil thing to wreak vengeance upon—a sort of
scapegoat for the sins of all creation!

Ever since that unfortunate incident in the garden of Eden the serpent has had heaped upon his
back the abiding enmity of the human race ; but this
is a mere trifle so far as the *cause* of the ill feeling
toward the reptile is concerned ; the real truth is, we
do not like his appearance or his ways, and we kill
him upon any and all occasions regardless of his his-
torical associations.

Now this is all wrong ; we must learn to let the
snake alone, or else in the long run we will be the
sufferers.   In this eastern part of the country we
have only two venomous snakes, the rattlesnake and
the copperhead ; all the rest are *absolutely harmless*.
As for these two dangerous reptiles, their venomous
character has been greatly overestimated, and a great
deal of sensational nonsense has been unnecessarily
connected with them through the credulity of the
ignorant.   Not more than two dogs in nine die who
have been bitten by the rattlesnake.*   The copperhead is by far a less venomous reptile than the other,
but to-day both are so rarely met with that they
scarcely deserve attention at all as familiar animals.

The rattlesnake still lives in some of the remote

---

* The Poison of Serpents.   S. Weir Mitchell.   The Century
Magazine, 1889, p. 514.

wildernesses of the northeastern States. In the
vicinity of Lake George, on one of the shores of
Lake Champlain, and perhaps in the southern Catskills, he is occasionally found; but in the Adirondack and White Mountains I believe he does not ex-
ist. In all the years that I have traveled among
these northern hills I have never met one, and I am
of the opinion that few, if any, are to be found to-
day even in those localities where they were once
reported to be plentiful.

Of the other harmless snakes, the racer, the water
snake, and the blowing adder are the most formidable
so far as *appearances* are concerned; but they are
only aggressive, and fight without doing much damage when angered. Not one of them can bite as
hard as the red squirrel, and they are not large
enough to seriously constrict a person. The racer
might possibly choke a child if he set about the task,
but I have only read of one instance where the reptile had sufficient courage to attempt anything on
quite so large a scale. As for our innocent little
green snake, he is the mildest and most defenseless
little animal on the face of the earth; the ringdove,
who is a creature to dread among the small birds, is a
monster compared with him.

Yet it is a fact only too familiar to us all that the
cry of "Snake!" on the highway is the immediate sig-

nal for war on the reptile with whatever weapons are handy—stones, pitchforks, clubs, sticks, or heels. Every man does his duty in the fray, and when the poor mutilated creature squirms at that part where he is not quite smashed, somebody remarks: " Oh, it isn't of any use to hit it any more ; you know snakes never die until after sundown " ; and we think so, or believe we do, and proceed on our way satisfied that the country is rid of one more big and dangerous reptile.

But what is the truth ? The farmer has lost one of his best friends; in proof of which, open the big snake's stomach and see what is there—mice, insects, grubs, slugs, rats, or moles, as the case may be ; all the worst enemies of the farmer. The very habits of the reptile are sufficient proofs of his harmless and beneficent character. He is never out at night, and in the spring he haunts the plowed fields and garden patches, ever on the alert for mice, or, best of all, grubs, cutworms, grasshoppers, and slugs. Yet in spite of all this the garden hoe is an ever-ready weapon with which to chase the poor thing from the field, if not to eventually make mince-meat of him.

It is a most curious fact that the greatest ignorance exists among many intelligent people regarding snakes. One would scout at believing such absurd things about any other kind of a creature, yet there

are many who think the snake exerts a sort of charm
over its prey; that a frightened mother snake
temporarily swallows her young in time of danger;
and that the forked tongue of the creature is its
deadly sting. Then one is told that a certain terrible
serpent of Africa rolls itself up like a hoople, chases
a man, and strikes him dead with its horny, spiked
tail. Also one is told that a snake never dies before
sunset; that it always licks its prey all over with its
forked tongue preparatory to swallowing it, so that it
will "slip down easily"; and that when its fangs are
extracted it lives an indefinite length of time on the
stimulus of its own poison, and without food, and so
on—*ad absurdum!*

But, as opposed to all this nonsense, I can cite a
number of *facts* not less remarkable and curious.
Snakes, for instance, are strangely tenacious of life;
some can and ·do live a while without their brains or
without their heart. The body decapitated for a certain length of time continues to move and coil, and
the separated head will dart out the tongue, or even
try to bite; * but I am not aware that these automatic
and convulsive movements are in any way checked by

---

* And more than this: Dr. S. Weir Mitchell says, " If we cut
off a snake's head and then pinch its tail, the stump of the neck
returns and with some accuracy hits the hand of the experimenter
—if he has the nerve to hold on!"—*Century Magazine, August,*
1889, p. 507.

the setting of the sun. When the last lingering remnants of life are fled the snake is dead, that is all. As for the tongue—that delicate and marvelously sensitive organ—it is absurd to think so soft a thing is a sting, and ridiculous to suppose it is adapted to licking; the snake is *dull of sight and hearing*, and this dainty tongue makes up for the deficiency by pursuing investigations by touch.

Snakes are, as a rule, remarkably prolific, and bear anywhere from seven to one hundred or more young. Sometimes the eggs of certain species hatch in the oviduct; hence the term ovoviviparous. It is easy to understand, therefore, that some ignorant person cutting open a snake in the early spring, and unaware of the true position of the stomach, should think that the creature had swallowed the young. But there are those who have very vague ideas of diseases as well as stomachs, and I remember a backwoodsman who during the greater part of one hot summer suffered terribly, according to his own account, from cholera infantum!

As for the swallowing process of the snake, that has a length which words can only inadequately measure. It is something like Milton's "linked sweetness long drawn out," without the sweetness. As a matter of fact, when one's teeth spread over one's palate it can not be expected that one's taste should escape being impaired. So it is with the snake: he may have a liking for birds, mice, and frogs, but that he can *taste* them is quite a different thing. A cobra in the London "Zoo" one time made a mistake and swallowed her blanket instead of a rabbit. It is true she was partially blind, as it was just before she should shed her skin,* but that fact in no wise affected her taste. It is therefore perfectly plain she could not distinguish the difference in flavor between rabbit fur and a blanket! To the average American snake a sleek young mouse is no more acceptable as a tidbit than a rank, acrid-skinned frog of the genus *Rana*.†

But the *way* the frog is swallowed is something

---

* At the time of sloughing, or casting the skin, snakes are partially blinded by the dull old skin which also covers the eye. It must be remembered that the ophidia do not possess eyelids.

† Even a snake is food for a snake. Here is a remarkable instance of such cannibalism. M. Léon Vaillant, in a paper read before the Académie des Sciences de Paris, says: "In a menagerie of the museum of the Jardin des Plantes, a French viper (*Pelias berus*) had to be put in the same cage with a horned viper (*Cerastes*). As the individuals, although they belonged to different species, were about the same size, it was supposed that they would live peaceably together. It was a mistake. During the night that followed the *Cerastes* swallowed the *Pelias*, and, in order to accommodate himself to his huge prey, his body was distended so that the scales which touched each other laterally and even lapped in his normal condition, were now so spread apart that between the longitudinal rows a bare space equal in size to the scales was left. Digestion went on regularly, however, and the *Cerastes* did not appear to suffer."—*The American Naturalist, March, 1893.*

appalling. It is one of those "ways" of the snake
which, as I have already said, we do not like. Now
we sometimes facetiously remark on the facility with
which a small boy "gets around" a large piece of pie.
The expression, however, more exactly fits the case
of the snake; he truly gets around his prey with a
courageous disregard for its formidable dimensions.
His head is scarcely half an inch thick, yet down
goes the frog between his distended jaws, and yet it
measured not a whit less than an inch and a half in
diameter. Now the simple fact is, the bones of the
serpent are held together by elastic ligaments, and
the reptile's capacity is correspondingly elastic. The
teeth, too, are set with a backward curve, and by
slightly working the jaws* the kicking frog is
worried down by slow degrees in spite of a slippery
hide which, were it not for those tiny, sharp, re-
curved teeth, might assist him in the struggle for
freedom. But he is doomed, and in less than ten
minutes his toes disappear, and he proceeds on a
lumpy course to the stomach of the reptile, smothered. Immediately after swallowing the frog the
snake gives a ghastly wide-mouthed gasp or two, as if
choking to death. But no such thing! he is merely

---

* These are formed of no less than four sections, two above
and two below, each of which is worked more or less independ-
ently.

working his jaws back to a state of repose, and gulping down a few breaths to make up for the time just past when breathing was somewhat difficult.

Like the batrachians, the snakes sleep all winter, waking up after a seven or eight months' nap under the vivifying influence of spring sunshine, and with a sharpened appetite for frogs, mice, and the like. At this time, too, the snake discards his dull skin and arrays himself in a resplendent coat of iridescent colors. The skin is shed complete, inside out, and scraped off by the contact with bushes, rough ground, and dead leaves.

Now the method of a snake's locomotion is as curious as its habit of hibernation. Watch one move, and it is hard to tell *how* he moves. We may think it is entirely by lateral pressure against every blade of grass and every grain of sand; but that is not all. The lithe creature does something more than push himself along. Every rib is employed in a measure as a leg would be, and with careful observation one may detect a certain undulation in wavelike intervals beneath the skin, which is due to the contraction and expansion of the ribs as the snake moves. Thus a snake can, if he chooses, move in almost a straight line and over rather slippery surfaces.

The constricting power of some snakes is also a marvel. With lightninglike rapidity the reptile will throw himself about the body of his victim and tighten his hold as one might tighten the cord about a bundle by pulling the string ends. But the squeezing of our American snakes is a more serious matter for mice than men, so we will pass that, and devote our attention to the snakes themselves.

There are two distinct groups or families of our snakes, one of which includes the poisonous rattlesnake and copperhead, and the other all the nonpoisonous snakes. Here they are as defined by Prof. S. F. Baird:

CROTALIDÆ: Erectible poisonous fangs in front; few teeth in the upper jaw; pupil of eye vertical; deep pit on the side of the face between the eye and nostril.

COLUBRIDÆ: No poisonous fangs; pupil of eye round; no pit, and both jaws fully provided with teeth.

According to Prof. Samuel Garman, there are at least four species of rattlesnakes east of the Mississippi River; but with one only will we have to do as a barely common object of familiar life. This is the Northern rattlesnake (*Crotalus horridus*).* Length, forty to sixty inches; dark brown above, blotched with brown, black, and tan somewhat diagonally;

---

* The nomenclature in every case is that of E. D. Cope, 1892. *Vide* Proc. U. S. Nat. Mu., vol. xiv, p. 589.

yellow beneath, blotched; contracted neck; carinated (keeled) dorsal scales in twenty-three to twenty-five rows. The fangs recline against the roof of the mouth protected by an elastic membrane. They are the only teeth on the maxillaries. These fangs when broken off or removed are replaced by others. The venom may or may not be ejected by the serpent.* Like the skunk, the creature is chary about dis-

The rattlesnake coiled to strike : showing the flattening of the body against the ground.

pensing what he seems to consider a valuable product not to be wasted on any account. The snake can only strike a distance equal to half the length of his body, and he is by no means aggressive, as the passer-by is unmolested if he does not begin hostilities. The snake need not necessarily be coiled to strike, either. He will throw himself right or left as far as the position of his body allows him to reach. The noise of the rattle is extremely like a rapid stridulation of the cone-headed grasshopper (*Conocephalus ensiger*), with

---

* Samuel Garman.

about eleven hundred vibrations to a minute, instead of two hundred and eighty-eight as in the case of the grasshopper.* Because a serpent may possess half a dozen sections to his rattle it by no means indicates that he is six years old. More than one section may be added in a year's time, and frequently one is broken off by accident.

The copperhead (*Ancistrodon contortrix*). Length, thirty-six inches; light rusty brown above, with darker blotches and a coppery cast to the head; ᴧ-shaped brown marks on sides; yellowish beneath; fangs like the rattlesnake's. An extremely rare but dangerous reptile, with a pointed, horny tail but with no warning rattle.

The familiar members of the non-poisonous family *Colubridæ* are as follows:

The ground snake (*Carphophiops amœnus*). Length, twelve inches; opalescent color; chestnut brown above, salmon beneath; head very small, not wider than the neck; thirteen dorsal rows;† found

---

* In the American Naturalist for March, 1893, somebody gives the vibrations of the rattle a tempo of one hundred and ten per minute. This is a great error, which may be proved at once by setting the metronome at one hundred and twelve —*adagio*.

† By this I mean that the scales on the back are arranged in thirteen rows.

under dry logs and stones in the mountains. Massachusetts to Louisiana and Illinois.

The worm snake* (*Carphophiops vermis*). Length, twelve inches; lustrous purple black above, flesh color beneath; colors about half and half; head very small, not wider than the neck; thirteen dorsal rows. Missouri, Kansas, and southern Illinois only.

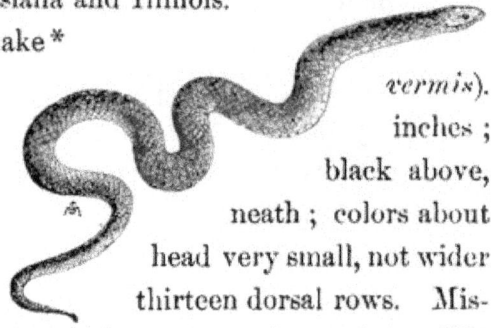

Ground snake, 12 inches.

The chain snake (*Ophibolus getulus getulus*). Length, forty-eight inches; handsome and inoffensive; black, crossed by narrow, continuous yellow—white rings which bifurcate on the flanks; on the back are large black hexagons; blotched with black beneath; head scarcely wider than the neck. Cope says that certain tamed chain snakes belonging once to his little daughter drank milk from a saucer. The chain snake is a great enemy to other

Chain snake, 48 inches.

---

* *Carphophis amœnus,* var. *vermis.* Samuel Garman.

snakes. Common in the South, and occasionally
found on Long Island, N. Y.; southern New York
to Florida and Louisiana.

The king snake (*Ophibolus getulus sayi*). Length,
forty-eight inches; black above, with a yellow spot on
each scale; the effect of these spots is to form sixty
transverse lines across the back; yellowish-white beneath, with black blotches. West of the Alleghanies,
north to Illinois and Wisconsin (Hoy).

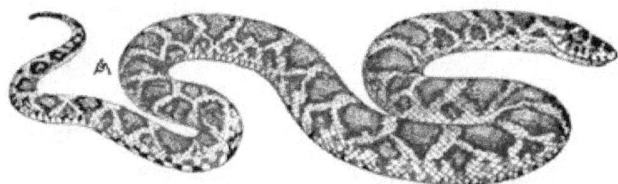

Milk snake, spotted adder, 48 inches.

The spotted adder, milk, or house snake (*Ophibolus doliatus triangulus*).* Length, forty-eight
inches; handsome; pale brown or ash-gray above,
with about fifty dorsal, transverse, triangular chocolate blotches edged with black; other lateral ones;
yellowish-white beneath, checkered with square black
blotches; small eye; twenty-one dorsal rows. It is
said to be fond of milk, and to frequent the floors of
dairies and cellars of houses. I killed one at least
thirty-eight inches long last summer in a vegetable

---

* He has even more names—viz., chicken snake, thunder and
lightning snake, checkered adder, etc.

garden, much against my will, but in deference to a
person who had a mortal antipathy to snakes. The
poor creature was absolutely harmless, and
never showed fight under the heavy blows
of a club. This was the first, and it will
be the last, harmless snake I shall accom-
modatingly kill for another—*transeat in
exemplum!* The milk snake is common from Maine to Virginia and
westward to Iowa and Wisconsin.

The ring-necked snake (*Diadophis
punctatus*). Length, fifteen inches; a
beauty, and dressed tastefully; violet-
black above, orange beneath, edged by
black spots; yellow-white ring or collar
around the neck; fifteen dorsal rows;
food, beetles, slugs, and grasshoppers;
found beneath fallen logs and stones.
Common in the mountains of Pennsylvania and Virginia, Maine to Wisconsin, and the Southern States.

The green or grass snake (*Liopeltis
vernalis; Cyclophis vernalis* of other
authors). Length, eighteen inches; beautiful; bright green above, yellowish beneath; fifteen dorsal rows; small head; *very smooth
scales;* food, insects, grubs, etc. Very common, and

Ring-necked
snake,
15 inches.

exceedingly gentle, frequenting wet meadows and sometimes climbing the alder bushes. My Manx cat frequently brought the pretty green creatures into my studio; they never showed the slightest hostility on being so roughly handled by the cat. Maine to Virginia and Wisconsin.

Another similar species (*Cyclophis æstivus*),* length, twenty-seven inches, has seventeen dorsal rows, the vertebral ones *strongly keeled ;* a long, slender Southern green snake. North to New Jersey and southern Illinois.

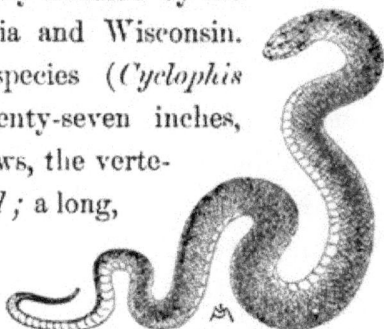

Green snake, 18 inches.

The fox snake (*Coluber vulpinus*). Length, sixty inches ; light brown above, with sixty dorsal, transverse chocolate blotches margined with black ; one or two lateral rows ; yellowish-white beneath ; the four lateral rows of scales smooth. Massachusetts to Kansas and northward.

The pilot snake, or mountain black snake (*Coluber obsoletus obsoletus*). Length, sixty inches ; graceful, inoffensive, and mild ; uniform silky brown or black above, with a few of the scales narrowly edged with white, slaty black beneath, with chin and throat yel-

---

* *Phyllophilophis æstivus.* Samuel Garman.

lowish; twenty-seven dorsal rows, the seven outer ones smooth. Resembles the racer, or black snake, in color only. Mt. Tom, Mass., to Texas; abundant in southern Illinois.

The pine, or bull snake (*Pityophis melanoleucus*). Length, sixty inches; very harmless; tan and buff; from twenty-seven to thirty-three dorsal blotches, brown margined with black; three series of lateral blotches; brownish-white beneath; twenty-nine dorsal rows. An exceedingly shy snake, frequenting sandy pine forests near the coast, and disappearing in a hole in the ground upon being surprised. Common south of the Ohio River, and found from New Jersey to South Carolina and Michigan (Gibbs).

The black snake, or racer (*Bascanium constrictor*). Length, forty-eight to eighty inches; lustrous black above, greenish or slaty-black beneath; chin and throat dull white; seventeen dorsal rows. An ugly

Black snake, racer,
48 inches.

customer when angered, but a harmless and cowardly one; remarkable for the speed with which it "covers the ground," and hence called "the racer." He frequents wild ground where there is water, climbs

trees with ease, and has a special penchant for birds
and their eggs.   He has no mean power of constric-
tion also, and wins in a fight with the rattlesnake.
Elliot Coues relates an instance in which he witnessed
one of the frequent combats between the black snake
and the rattlesnake, when the former, in less time than
it takes to tell it, snapped the latter asunder by wind-
ing the anterior and posterior parts of his body around
the neck and tail of the rattlesnake and suddenly pulling himself taut.   The food of this snake is mainly
rats, mice, frogs, toads, and birds.   Not uncommon
throughout the country east of the Missouri River.

The striped, or ribbon snake (*Eutania saurita*).*
Length, twenty-eight inches ; light, bright chocolate above, with three yellow stripes ; greenish-white
beneath ; nineteen dorsal rows ; large eyes ; slender
and graceful figure, agile ; found on the edge of the
woods or near the water.   A mild-tempered creature,
which, should it happen to bite, pricks one's finger as
a pin might.   Common throughout the east, and
abundant in the Alleghany mountains.

The western garter, or striped snake (*Eutania
radix*).   Length, twenty inches ; brownish or green-
ish-black above, with three narrow yellow stripes, and
six series of black spots, sometimes obscure ; pale

---

* These striped or garter snakes emit an offensive odor.

greenish tone beneath, marked black; nineteen dorsal rows, sometimes less. Common in central Western States to Lake Michigan and Oregon.

The common garter snake (*Eutænia sirtalis sirtalis*). Length, thirty to forty inches; olive-brown above, sometimes nearly black, with three narrow light-yellow stripes encroached upon by the three series of small black spots on sides; greenish white beneath; nineteen dorsal rows; dorsal scales keeled; body somewhat stout; food, frogs, toads, mice, etc.; stouter than *Eutænia saurita*. This snake is commoner in New York than any other species. It is found from Essex County to Westchester County, and I remember it as the most familiar snake about Lake Mahopac, Putnam County. It frequents wet meadows, and is generally found near the water. The female bears a great number of young; she is ovoviviparous.

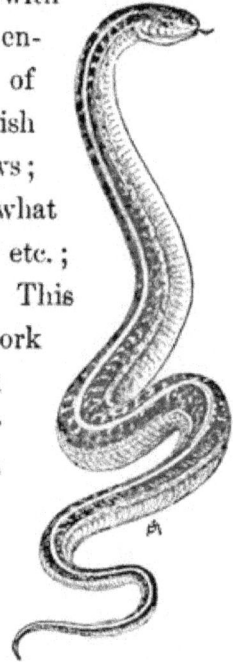

Garter snake, 30 inches.

Professor Baird says he has killed one with no less than eighty-three little ones about six inches long. It is a disagreeable snake to handle, as it emits a fetid odor. Common through the United States, excepting the Pacific coast; but I have not yet seen one in the White Mountain region; it evidently prefers a warmer climate. It is abundant, however, in Illinois.

Still another species of the garter snake (*Eutænia sirtalis dorsalis*) is common throughout the United States. This species is brownish olive above, with three broad green-white stripes, dark spots on the sides, and greenish white beneath.

The brown, or spotted snake (*Storeria dekayi*). Length, twelve inches; ash or chestnut-brown above, with a clay-colored dorsal band, dotted along the margin two scales apart; gray-white beneath; a dark patch on either side of the back of the head; seventeen dorsal rows; food, insects, etc. Exceedingly common in New York and Massachusetts; abundant on the shores of Lake Champlain. Maine to Wisconsin, Florida, and Texas.

The red-bellied snake (*Storeria occipitomaculata*). Length, twelve inches; pretty; ash, chestnut, or even olive-brown above, with three distinct light-colored irregular spots behind the head; a beautiful reddish-salmon beneath; fifteen dorsal rows; dorsal scales keeled;

Red-bellied snake, 12 inches.

food, insects, etc. Very abundant everywhere on meadows and grassy ground, and associated with *Storeria dekayi*. Maine to Florida and Texas.

Kirtland's snake (*Clonophis kirtlandi; Tropido-clonium kirtlandi* of other authors). Length, sixteen inches; a beauty; light, ruddy brown above, with three alternating series of round black spots, the central ones of which are indistinct and the smallest; reddish or perhaps yellowish beneath, with a row of small black spots on either side; nineteen dorsal rows; body stout. It will flatten its body and remain motionless to escape detection. A Western snake. Ohio to Illinois.

The water snake or water adder (*Natrix fasciata sipedon; Nerodia sipedon* of other authors). Length, forty eight inches; dull bronze brown above, redder on the sides; transverse light irregular bands margined with black; yellowish to reddish beneath; twenty-three dorsal rows; head

Water snake, 48 inches.

narrow and long; strongly carinated scales. This snake frequents marshes, overflowed meadows, and the shores of streams and ponds, climbs among the

bushes, coils there, and slips into the water when
alarmed; it is a good swimmer, and a great fighter
when enraged, but it is perfectly harmless.   It is
the cast skin of this reptile which that interesting
woodland bird, the crested flycatcher (*Myiarchus
crinitus*), is so fond of as a lining for her nest.*

The food of the water adder is
frogs, small fish, salamanders, etc.
Common from Massachusetts to Wisconsin and Georgia.   In
the South it is called
the water moccasin.

Another species of water
snake, sometimes called the
queen snake (*Natrix leberis; Regina leberis* of other
authors), length, twenty-
three inches, also common
in the East, is differently marked; the color above
is chestnut- or chocolate-brown, with a lateral yellow band and three narrow black dorsal stripes; yellowish beneath; nineteen dorsal rows; dorsal scales
carinated.   Frequents the banks of streams, and shallow water where there are loose stones.   Common

Queen snake, 23 inches.

---

* The nest is usually in a hole fifteen feet up in a tree, and it
is lined with bits of roots, grasses, and snake's skin.

from New York to Wisconsin; abundant in the
mountains of Pennsylvania and Ohio.

The blowing or deaf adder or hognose (*Heterodon
platyrhinus*).   Length, thirty inches; yellow-gray
and sepia-brown above, checkered with about thirty
dark dorsal blotches; yellowish beneath; a dark band
across the forehead, and a pug nose; strongly carinated scales back of the head; twenty-five dorsal
rows.   This beggar has a threatening aspect when we
approach him, but he is perfectly harmless; he is "all
bark and no bite," flattening his head and body out
until he looks twice as big as he really is, and hissing
like a steam engine, with an effect of fearful malig-
nancy.   He is the creature, too, who, so hard of hearing, was the occasion of that familiar and suggestive

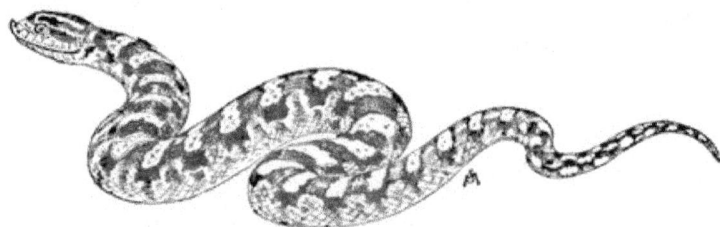

Hognose snake, blowing adder, 30 inches.

saying, "as deaf as an adder."   He is common through
the Eastern and Southern States, is rare in New
York, and probably is not found at all in New England.

The hognose snake (*Heterodon simus*).   Length,

twenty-six inches; stouter and smaller than *II. pla-tyrhinus*; light brown-yellow, with a dorsal series of thirty-five transverse black blotches; sides with one to three smaller series; yellowish beneath; twenty-three to twenty-seven dorsal rows; a decided pug nose, evidently of great use in burrowing through the soil. Common in the West and South.

CHAPTER V.

ACCOMPLISHED VOCALISTS.

The Robin, Hermit Thrush, Veery, Redstart, Wood Pewee, etc.

ALL the strange world of wild life offers no greater contrast than that between the snake and the bird. The latter is a true musician; the former is as mum as the brown leaf under which he hides. Who has heard the robin's note and failed to recognize the fact that the bird is a musician?

I do not make a random selection of the robin (*Merula migratoria*) among the long list of singing birds, and intimate that he is a musician beyond the rest. Many a woodland bird is a better singer; but to every thrush's song we will hear a score of robins' songs, and some one of the robins will most likely be an accomplished vocalist, just like the one whose music I have interpreted a little farther on.

We respond to the musical side of Nature only in proportion to the development of our "ear for music." It must be admitted that this very common expres-

7   81

sion implies that there are those who have *no* ear for music—those, in other words, who are tone-deaf. But tone-deafness is simply a qualifying term, and we are forced to admit that the person without an ear for music is to a certain extent deaf. Now, a partially deaf person will hardly be able to distinguish apart the songs of two different robins, one of which is much more musical than the other. So I must appeal to the imagination of the unmusical as well as the musical mind in order to have my bird songs understood; they must not be taken too literally.*

I have said that we respond to the music of Nature according to the degree of our musical perception; but it only needs a little cultivation of our sense of hearing to be able to intelligently grasp the musical idea which Nature is constantly suggesting. Thus a musical robin last June sang the following melody, more or less perfectly:

---

* Without imagination it would be difficult, if not impossible, to understand a wild bird's song. One has not only to hear all the notes with an attentive ear, but sort them out, so to speak, and transmute them to truer and better conditions. Thus, what is doubtfully A in a bird's song must be positively A in the hearer's mind; and a musical fifth which is *off* a quarter or half a tone must be considered—not a bit off! In music we allow only tones and half-tones—for instance, C and D; between the two is C sharp, the half-tone. The bird is very apt to sing a quarter-tone, that is something halfway between C and C sharp.

But this song was suggestive rather than positive; the robin produced all the melody, but it was a vague melody. One could not be quite positive that every turn was meant to be just what the musical mind demanded that it *ought* to be.

Nature is always suggesting, but never completing; she does not commit herself to measured tones and exact musical phrases any more than she does to exact primary colors. It is invariably that vagueness of purport that renders her work fascinating, and inspires the artist to take hold of it and make the meaning plain.

There is no doubt in my mind that the robin tried to touch as many tones of regular intervals as he could. Certainly he had more excuse for errors than the unmusical man who vowed that he could always distinguish "My country, 'tis of thee," from "Yankee Doodle." But who, pray, would call the robin unmusical that could produce such a melody as that I have transcribed? Without interpretation, his song, although jerky, agitated, and vague in meaning, would still be perfectly musical. I have taken no liberties with his triplets.

But here is another specimen from a sprightly musician who sang in a maple tree for a few minutes one day last June, just before my studio window (in Campton, N. H.), and then disappeared

never   to   return.
It was a Baltimore
oriole (*Icterus gal-*
bula), and his simple musical phrase was absolutely
true in pitch, differing in this respect from my
robin's song. But the most remarkable thing about
a really musical oriole—one may not happen to be as
melodic as another—is the way he syncopates. Now
syncopation in music is equivalent to the dropping of
an important note; one of accent or emphasis. Who
has not heard in the streets the shrill fife and drum
with the measured boom of the bass drum, and who
does not remember the turn the latter makes at the
end of a musical phrase? It sounds as though the
next to the last "boom" was dropped in the street,
and the drummer, stooping to pick it up, lost a little
time and then hurriedly made it up thus: Boom!
boom! boom! boom! boom! boom! boom!——
boom-boom!

This is a perfect syncope, and it is exactly what
the whistling oriole is continually doing. Here is a
second instance of dropped notes in a little song I
once heard in the Harvard Botanical Garden, Cambridge, in May.

But this oriole
was not quite so musical as the one I heard in Campton, N. H.

THE BANKS
OF THE
PEMIGEWASSET,
THE HOME OF THE
BLACK-BILLED CUCKOO.

COCCYZUS
ERYTHROPHTHALMUS.

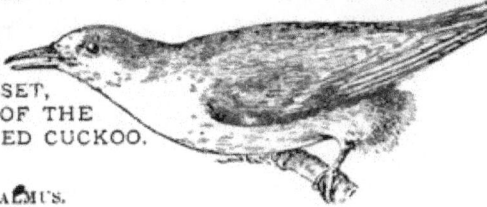

I have long since learned who plays the "kettle-drum" of the bird orchestra; he is the black-billed cuckoo (*Coccyzus erythrophthalmus*) a long, lithe, pigeonlike creature, who is subject to nervous attacks after a prolonged silence, and lets off the following:

But the black-billed cuckoo does not confine himself to exactly this arrangement of his two notes. Sometimes he sings thus:

It is also not quite fair to liken him to a noisy drummer. His note is more resonant than that of the tubby kettledrum, and as a musician he is the soul of accuracy in his musical thirds and fourths. But the mention of this reminds me of the musical attempts of the crow. I wonder how many of us have caught the crow in the act of coughing up a number of musical tones! It is the most absurd performance in all the category of wild music. The crow when he sings is nothing short of a clown. He ruffles his feathers, stretches his neck like a cat with a fishbone in her throat, and with a most tremendous effort delivers a series of henlike squawks double *fortissimo*, thus:

What he means by the call it is difficult to say, unless it has some connection with the general "caucus" which

is sure to be in full session at no great distance down
in the copse on the meadow border.   But the crow
is not unmusical after all.
His "caw" is a note
of decisive emphasis
which can not be justly
slighted in the grand
orchestra of Nature. The
tone of it has that wood-
en, reedlike quality which
is best represented by the oboe,
an instrument of a singularly pastoral
nature.   Haydn fully appreciated this
fact, and in his oratorio of The Seasons
gave it a very prominent position not
only in a fine *adagio*, but in a long
solo imitating the crowing of a rooster.

The musical Crow.

Notice how nicely the notes follow
the last part of the "crow" by sliding down the
chromatic scale.

Here is a case
where a great
musician followed the suggestion of Nature very
closely; and I could enumerate several others in
which Nature's intention was most admirably carried
out.   However, I can only record one extreme instance, which is as pathetic as it is interesting; and

THE YELLOWHAMMER.

COLAPTES AURATUS.

"On the wooded border of a meadow."

whenever I hear the golden-winged woodpecker's
(yellow-hammer's) nasal and monotonous voice, I remember how *much* Beethoven made of it in his Pastoral Symphony.   In the summer of 1823, long after
the great composer had become "stone deaf," he was
walking with his friend Schindler on the wooded
border of a meadow not far from Vienna.   "Seating
himself on the grass," says Schindler, "and leaning
against an elm, Beethoven asked me if any yellow-
hammers were to be heard in the tree above us.
But all was still.   He then said, 'This is where I
wrote The Scene by the Brook,* while the yellow-
hammers were singing above me, and the quails,
nightingales, and cuckoos calling all around.'   I
asked why the yellow-hammer did not appear in
the movement with the others; on which he seized
his sketchbook and wrote the following phrase:

 'There's the little composer,' said
he, 'and you'll find that he plays
a more important part than the
others, for they were nothing but a joke.'"

Well, the power of a musician's imagination to
transmute a few tones is illimitable, for the notes
above are not those of the yellow-hammer at all.
But, as I have already intimated, imagination is neces-

* Die Scene am Bach, the second movement of the sixth (Pastoral) symphony.

sary on the part of the hearer to understand the musical drift of Nature. So Beethoven gives his imagination full play, and constructs a part of his symphony not from the yellow-hammer's monotonous
"kee-er, kee-er" alone,
but from the association
of these vigorous tones
with the milder ascending tones of still another bird
—the nightingale, perhaps.

To my mind Beethoven's six notes and others
like them of constant recurrence in The Scene by
the Brook are remarkably suggestive of the hermit
thrush (*Turdus aonalaschkæ pallasii*), our most
gifted American songster—the *prima donna* of the
orchestra. The notes of this bird always fly upward
with bounding emphasis to some extremely high point,
and after a short interval these three very high notes
succeed, followed by a whispered "wee-
chee-weechee" too attenuated for me to
record by musical signs.

Much has been written about the music
of the hermit thrush, but I have found nothing which
treats the bird with justice except the remarkably
faithful records jotted down by Mr. Simeon Pease
Cheney.* It is almost exclusively to this gifted mu-

---

* Author of Wood Notes Wild; he died May 10th, 1890.

sician, who has lived among the birds in the green
hills of Vermont, that we are indebted for any scientific knowledge of bird music.

In a previous volume * I have devoted some attention to the songs of the thrushes, and have given
a song of the hermit thrush which is almost identical
with one reported by Mr. Cheney. It is characterized by thirds and triplets. Here is a portion of it:

But this is only one phase, although a very common
one, of the hermit's music. He can do even
better than that, and be- sides a number of most extraordinarily clear silvery whistles, he gives us a subdued,
reedlike series of *pianissimo*
tones which I can only liken
to those of a
harmonicon.

It is very
likely that this peculiar nature of these *pianissimo* notes—
they can not be heard more than
forty feet away — suggested to

The Hermit Thrush.

---

* Familiar Features of the Roadside.

Burroughs the hymnlike quality of the hermit's song which he so often mentions. I must quote what he says: "A strain has reached my ears from out the depths of the forest that to me is the finest sound in nature—the song of the hermit thrush. . . . It appeals to the sentiment of the beautiful in me, and suggests a serene religious beatitude as no other sound in nature does. It is perhaps more of an evening than a morning hymn, though I hear it at all hours of the day. It is very simple, and I can hardly tell the secret of its charm. 'O spheral, spheral!' he seems to say; 'O holy, holy! O clear away, O clear away!' interspersed with the finest trills and the most delicate preludes."

But this is the sentiment of the song; what of the song itself? That I can only describe with musical annotations. There is first a prolonged tone, probably A; this is succeeded by another shorter one a third above, another a fifth above, and still another an octave above the A. Interspersed are several very short notes, which are undoubtedly some of Burroughs's "fine trills and delicate preludes." Here is the music: But we will notice that the song does not end with the high note; there are still three more which glide downward, finishing at the original A; these have that harmonicon quality of which I have spoken. So pronounced is this final harmonic tone that it might well be expressed thus:

Now, this is but one of six musical phrases which a single bird sang. Another, but a less gifted musician, sang a similar phrase.

 But, of all the singers, not one, however clear - voiced, equaled in dexterity and precision the bird I heard last summer, which sang the following:

 The distinctness and rapidity of the last six short notes was simply phenomenal; they furnished a fitting cadenza to a long song of certainly eight or nine passages not one of which was like an- other. After the bird finished his solo—in a maple tree not ten yards from where I sat —he fluttered silent- ly away to a neigh- boring brook to "wet his whistle."

The Veery.

Wholly unlike the her- mit's music is that of the skulking veery (*Turdus fuscescens*), who haunts the shrubbery by the river's brink, and leaves the hillside grove entirely to his

more accomplished musician cousin. Still, the veery's
song is the most romantic and suggestive one of the
twilight hour in spring. His notes are characterized
by a reedlike quality, which I will liken again to the
tones of a harmonicon. No other bird has a voice
like his; it can best be imitated by humming a low
tone and whistling a high one; and it sounds as
though the little owner was being swung in four suc-
cessive circles through the air. Somebody has compared its character to that of a spiral line. Notice
after the preliminary grace notes the unbroken flow
of the four clusters which follow :

No hermit could do that sort of thing as well; he
would not have breath enough. But there is also
another than spiral effect to this musician's song.
Sometimes a rare individual sings whose sonorous
tones vibrate be-
tween thirds and
fifths, thus :

And in a chorus of veeries such as I heard last spring
his notes stand out by contrast with the others in a
most refreshing way; let one's ear be never so subtle
at following a musical cadence, it can not be quick
enough to catch the full beauty of the last notes of

this eccentric singer; they must be heard over and
over again to be remembered. They remind one of
the weird effect of an æolian harp or a singing telegraph pole,* but they are twice as mysterious.

But the most mysterious singer of the woodland
is the chipper and restless little redstart (*Setophaga
ruticilla*), whose jet-black
head and orange shoul-
ders are continually
perking out from the
bordering green of the
highway, and surprising one
by a sudden and transient

The Redstart.

glimpse of bright color. This little fellow does not
perch on the tree-top like the indigo bird and the
song sparrow when he sings; he evades the public
eye, and chirrups on the other side of the tree from
the inquisitive observer. His song, much more
sprightly than that of the veery, and much less serious, runs thus: He is ever
on the alert for an in-
sect, and never hesitates to

Che-we che-we-we-we che-weo.

cut his song short when a tempting mouthful meets
his eye in the shape of some "crawly bug" on a

---

* In extremely cold weather, if one's ear is placed against the
telegraph pole one will hear a remarkable harmonic vibration of
the wires, like that of an æolian harp.

leaf near by. The "ching a-wee, cher-wee, wee—!" quite as often ends abruptly as otherwise, and there is one less insect in the shrubbery.

A still more mysterious singer in the wildwood, one who sings along with the hermit thrush and who has ever evaded my watchful eyes, is the wood pewee (*Contopus virens*). I have seen fifty thrushes to one pewee, and yet have heard both singing at the same time and in the same wood. At last, in the past season, I saw the pewee: a plainly attired little creature, with rusty black back and gray-white breast. There he was, on a sprig of the gray birch, calling his mate, as usual, with "Sally, come here! H-e-r-e!" but musically, thus:

Sally come here   Here!

It is the most musical of calls, full of suggestiveness, and quite as much a part of the spring orchestra as the peep of the *Hyla*. But the most remarkable part of it is the long-drawn-out "H-e-r-e!" which might just as well be translated "Whi-e-e-eu!" It is a whistle rapidly descending the scale, precisely like the whistle of painful surprise one makes when one's "best corn" is trodden on. In the case of the bird

the prolonged note of surprise is, I am always thinking, an indication of his unbounded amazement at
the unnecessary delay in obeying his peremptory
summons.   He keeps up this whistling for his wife
all summer long; the only answer he seems to get
comes from the borders of a neighboring field.   It is
the call of the chickadee:

Pe-wee. Fiddl'de de.

CHAPTER VI.

STRANGE CREATURES WITH STRANGE VOICES.

The Bittern, Owl, Loon, etc.

A STRANGE sound comes from the meadow swamp down by the pond—" *G-chug, g-chug, g-chug.* It is the uncanny voice of the bittern or stake-driver (*Botaurus lentiginosus*), and if we could *see* him making the noise we would exclaim at once, " That bird is beastly ill!" Such a remarkable performance one never witnessed; the distressing musical attempt of the crow recorded in the preceding chapter is not a circumstance to this convulsive proceeding of the bittern. He " hiccoughs " wildly several times, and then is apparently seized with a most violent fit of nausea, producing with each convulsion a hollow " booming " noise which on most occasions sounds like somebody driving a stake in the ground. This charming music I suppose the naturalist would call the love-song of the bird; it is certainly most common in April, and its continuance for half an hour or more is perhaps accounted for by the indifference of the female, who possibly considers the noise too unattractive for a prompt response. Indeed, it is on record that the bird has "pumped" for an hour. The sucking sound of a pump, I might explain, is considered by some the nearest ·approach to this strange creature's unmusical notes.

If we are near enough to the swamp where the bittern stands, we will see a bird, about twenty-four inches high, with a slate-gray head and neck—the latter black-streaked—and a brown back, standing upright and motionless. It really takes quite a sharp eye to separate the bird from his surroundings. When he moves, his deliberate and stealthy steps are hardly perceptible; but as soon as he opens his bill to speak his strange actions attract our notice and enlist our sympathy.

His crop is seemingly distended with air which he has swallowed in a most noisy fashion; every time he takes a gulp of it the head is thrown upward and then forward, the body is violently convulsed, and, with every feather puffed out, one imagines the wretched creature is at his last gasp with a torturing fishbone in his throat.

But no; he is only singing his *chant d'amour*, or amusing himself with a bit of everyday vocal athletics. Mr. William Brewster, of Cambridge, describes the sound as a trisyllabic one, thus: *Pump-er-*

8

lunk, *pump-er-lunk*, etc.   Evidently his bird was a
"pumper"; but all the bitterns that I have heard
were "stake-drivers," and sang thus,
the second syllable closely resembling
the resounding *thwack* of a woodman's
axe as it drives some stout stake in the ground.

The bird begins operations by raising his head and
stretching his neck until the bill is pointed up in the
air; then with three or four preliminary snaps of the
bill, which can be heard fully five hundred feet away,
off he goes on his *g-chug, g-chug, g-chug, g-chug,*
from four to eight times, when he tires of it and takes
a minute to rest; then—*da capo.*

Thoreau alludes to this remarkable bird thus:
"The stake-driver is at it again on his favorite
meadow.   I followed the sound and at last got within
two rods.   When thus near, I heard some lower
sounds at the beginning like striking on a stump or a
stake, a dry, hard sound, and then followed the gur-
gling, pumping notes. . . . I went to the place, but
could see no water."   It seems Thoreau, like a good
many others, imagined that the bird made the noise
with the help of water—by partly submerging his
bill.   But all who know the stake-driver and his
strange performance now agree that water has nothing to do with the case.

I have heard and seen the bird on the river

THE BITTERN.

BOTAURUS LENTIGINOSUS.

"The stake-driver is at it again on
his favorite meadow."

meadows of Grafton County, N. H., and I know that
he makes the noise when there is not a bit of water
in his vicinity. Bradford
Torrey records a most interesting performance of a bittern which he witnessed in
company with Mr. Walter
Faxon,* and he declares that
the bird was perched on
the dry remnants of an old
haystack. He furthermore
says the sounds are not entirely caused by an exertion
of the vocal organs, but are
connected in some way with
the distention of the crop
and the drawing in of the
breath, *not* the throwing of
it out after the crop is full.

In the dim twilight suc-
ceeding a warm day in spring

The Great Horned Owl.

another strange but familiar note comes across the
meadow from the edge of the bordering wood, and
we recognize at once the hoot of an owl. It is a
barytone note, and from its depth and freedom from

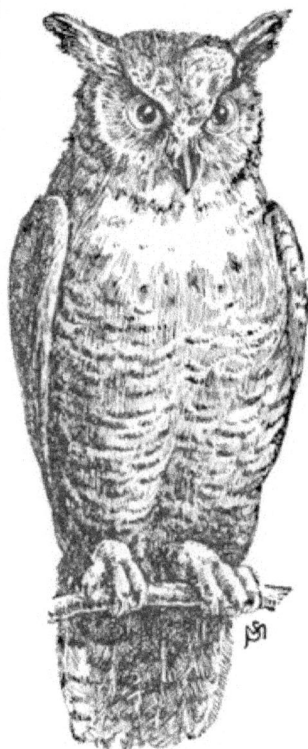

* The Auk, vol. vi, p. 1.

a quivering, weird quality (familiar in the screech-owl's notes), we can be sure it comes from one of the larger owls. It is, in fact, the voice of the great horned owl (*Bubo virginianus*), a big, brown-and-ocher-colored bird, mottled with black, and remarkable for his tufted ears, the conspicuous feathers on which stand out fully two inches beyond the contour of his head.

Mr. Frank M. Chapman calls this owl, just as many another ornithologist does, "a tiger among birds." The creature is a terror to small birds, poultry, squirrels, mice, and rabbits. But he is not quite so destructive to the inmates of the henhouse as he is made out to be. On the average, not more than one owl in four steals a chicken; all the others feed on mice, moles, and other such harmful creatures which live on the farm.

One of the first voices of spring is that of the horned owl; it is not a cheerful one, but it is a presage of warm days to come, and is therefore welcome. Here are the notes of an owl I heard hooting in May last:

There is but one dominant tone to the song; my grace-notes, of course, only indicating a certain modulation of the voice, do not indicate a second tone. One of the most extreme instances of modulation in a bird's voice is mani-

fested in that of the loon (*Urinator imber*), whose
sliding note resembles that outrageous invention
called a "siren" whistle, which one may hear any
time in the harbor of New York. I do not mean to
imply by this comparison that the loon when he calls
sprawls all over the chromatic scale, as the above-
mentioned whistle does; he does not; the screech
owl comes far nearer that sort of thing. But the
loon *does* modulate his "O-ho-oo!"
in a wild, *fortissimo* way so nearly like
the "siren" that the comparison, to my
mind, is a very natural one. Mr. Cheney's rendering of the three notes is different;
but all birds do not sing alike.

I quote what Mr. J. H. Langille
says of the loon's voice. "Beginning on the fifth
note of the scale, the voice slides through the eighth
to the third of the scale above in loud, clear, sonorous
tones, which on a dismal evening before a thunder-
storm—the lightning already playing along the inky
sky—are anything but musical." Here they are:
"He has also another but rather soft and
pleasing utterance, sounding like 'Who-
who-who-who,' the syllables being so
rapidly pronounced as to sound almost like a shake of
the voice—a sort of weird laughter."

This last calmer but still strong cry is usually uttered while the bird is on the wing; it runs thus:

Hoo-oo-o-o-o hoo-oo-o-o-o oo-o-o-o.

Many years ago the weird song was a very familiar one to me at the twilight hour in the wilderness of the Adirondacks. I do not know whether the loon to-day frequents the lakes, which thirty years ago were his favorite haunts; I do not think he does. The changes in the woods are radical, and civilization has introduced numberless fashionable and elaborate " camps," which prove most conclusively that there is less venison, trout, and loon music there than there used to be in the " sixties."

The loon is a retiring character, who avoids all contact with the civilized world and lives in the seclusion of the wilderness. In 1887 Mr. Simeon Pease Cheney found ample opportunity to study the loon at Trout Lake, St. Lawrence County, N. Y., about twenty-five miles northwest of Paul Smith's. According to his account, the nest of a certain loon he saw was simply a cavity in some dry muck on the ruins of an old muskrat house. The female, he explains, shoved herself on it very much as she pushed herself into the water, and did not, as Wilson says, approach it on the wing by darting obliquely and falling securely in it. Loons never lay more than two grayish, olive-brown eggs speckled with black, and these are nearly as large (three and a half inches long) as those of a goose.

The loon is a big bird, anywhere from twenty to thirty-two inches long from bill to tail, and so characteristically aquatic that he is absolutely helpless and clumsy on land ; the legs are too far back to be of any service in walking, and when on the shores of a lake he shoves himself forward partly on his breast. I have heard sportsmen say that it was next to impossible to shoot one of the creatures ; he must be struck in

The Loon.

the head or not at all, as the feathers on the body are so thick and close that the shot is effectually checked by them ; besides that, as an escaping diver the bird is without an equal. He disappears upon the slightest provocation, swims under the water an

extraordinary distance, and reappears far away, on the other side of the lake, perhaps, quite out of gun-shot. The following is Mr. Cheney's description of an alarmed loon's method of progression on the sur-face of the water: "Suddenly there was a furious dashing and splashing just behind us, and in a mo-ment more one of them rushed by very near us, both flying and swimming, with wings in the air and feet in the water. He swept by us with a noise like a steamboat, but no boat could equal his speed. At every stroke of his wings he smote the water as well as the air."

But aquatic birds are always a source of surprise to us when we see the rapidity of their progression through the water. Last June, when the Pemige-wasset River, New Hampshire, had swollen to an enormous and resistless flood after a long rain, and I was watching the seething water sweeping beneath the bridge with fearful rapidity, I was much sur-prised to witness the successful efforts of a red-breasted sheldrake (*Merganser serrator*) making *up-stream* with no inconsiderable amount of speed. I shouted and clapped my hands, and the bird, taking immediate alarm, flapped his wings and shot over the surface of the flying water like an express train. I calculated at the time he was making fully thirty miles an hour, although relatively with the river bank

THE PEMIGEWASSET RIVER,
AT BLAIR'S BRIDGE, AND
THE SHELDRAKE.

MERGANSER SERRATOR.

" He slyly proceeds
up stream."

his speed did not count for so much. At ordinary
times, when the river is low, I have seen this wild
duck propel himself noisily through the water with a
rapidity that would rival the best effort of a Harvard
oarsman.

On being alarmed the sheldrake utters a melan-
choly, hoarse "quonk," usually in the key of C.
His voice is often heard late in
the afternoon, when with his fellows he shyly proceeds upstream
in quest of the little fish that abound in the river.
He pursues and captures his prey under the water,
and, like the loon, dives upon the slightest disturbance which occurs near his retreat.

Merganser serrator is a red-breasted sheldrake,
whose white-ringed neck and broad band of rust
color on the upper breast, black streaked, distinguish
him from the other species, *Merganser americanus*,
whose breast is white tinged with salmon.

A group of sheldrakes on a quiet bit of the river
is an interesting gathering to stir up. Occasionally
one or two individuals make some passing remark
—probably on the possible presence of an observer in
the vicinity. The ducks keep a sharp lookout both
for fish and men ; suddenly some one springs out of
the neighboring thicket with an abrupt shouting and
clapping of hands ; instantly the river in the vicinity

of the ducks is a scene of wildest turmoil and confusion, the ducks flee, and the water is rapidly churned up for a quarter of a mile downstream. In less than a minute after all is quiet again, and no one would think there was a duck within a hundred miles of the spot.

So we turn from the lonesome river brink and direct our footsteps to the wood on the hillside; hardly have we stepped within its shade when there is the greatest commotion among the ferns and the dead leaves, where a hen and her chickens have been hiding; they scatter in all directions. But it was a partridge hen, and she has as much trouble in collecting her faculties as her " chicks," for we can still hear her excited, nervous clucks in the distance. I once came upon such a brood so suddenly and noiselessly that one of the little things was nearly beneath my foot before my intrusion was discovered. With an experimental turn of mind I immediately began to chirp like a lost chicken, and in an instant the distracted mother came tearing back to the rescue; for a few moments she stood directly before me in the most anxious attitude, and, making the most distressful clucks and cries, tried to regain her lost chick. But she was shortly convinced that I was a base deceiver, and left as hurriedly as she came.

The partridge (*Bonasa umbellus*) is responsible

for some of the strangest noises that break the stillness of the mountain forest. The female is always
clucking and quirping on the approach of an intrud-
ing footstep, and she never seems to discover it until it is within a couple of
yards of her re- treat. I should
imagine, not only from this
circum- stance but from the
fact that the male
bird makes such a rum-
pus in spring when he
calls his mate, that she is a
bit deaf. One almost treads
upon the tail of a partridge

The Partridge.

before it occurs to the creature to get out of the
way; then there is a fearful *whir-r-r-r-r*, violent
and startling enough to set one's heart beating, and
the bird is gone, not, however, without making the
following vocal exclamation,
whistled in a variety of tones
as shrill and explosive as some
of the remarks of the red squirrel. I always imagine
the bird saying, "Why in thunder didn't you say you
were coming? it's a shocking surprise!"

But this chick-o'-the woods is no fool; he knows
he can make noise enough to rattle the sportsman,
shake his nerves, and spoil his aim, so he does not

hurry himself to move off. His mottled brown colors are amply protective, and if he "lies low" he can save himself the trouble of an arduous retreat on the wing. Partridges do not care to fly if they can avoid it. Indeed, a glance at my drawing of the wing shows that it is not the best shape for flying. Compared with the pigeon's wing * it is short and stumpy, although handsome.

Wing of the partridge.

The strangest noise the partridge makes may be heard in the spring; then the male bird mounts an old stump or a log and begins his "crow" in the usual way, but his voice is silent. He beats his wings exactly as the rooster does, but with an expert's ability, and does no more. *Thump, thump, thump, thump, thump, thump, th-ur-r-r-r-r-r-r-r !*

The tone is that of a muffled snare drum. He is unquestionably the drummer of Nature's orchestra.

---

* The carrier pigeon has been known to fly one hundred miles in an hour.

The great question among naturalists has always been *how* he made the noise. I think the question has not long since been answered by more than one observer, and one of the best of these answers has come from Mr. Cheney. I quote what he says: " It is now plainly to be seen that the performer stood straight up, like a junk bottle, and brought his wings in front of him with quick, strong strokes, smiting nothing but the air, not even his 'own proud breast,' as one distinguished observer has suggested. . . . The first two or three thumps are soft and comparatively slow, then they increase rapidly in force and frequency, rushing onward into a furious whir, the whir subsiding in a swift but graduated diminish. The entire power of the partridge must be thrown into this exercise. His appearance immediately afterward affirms it as strongly as does the volume of sound, for he drops into the forlornest of attitudes, looking as if he would never move again. In a few minutes, however—perhaps five—he begins to have nervous motions of the head; up, up, it goes, and his body with it, till he is perfectly erect—legs, body, neck, and all. Then for the thunder once more."

I can add nothing to this perfect description of the performance. The noise *is* made, just as has been stated, by the wings beating the air with furious rapidity. There should be no doubt whatever about

that, and all I need to produce a convincing proof of
the fact is a machine that will vibrate a pair of wings,
which I have before me as I write, at the rate of five
hundred times a minute.   Hollow the hands and then
clap them rapidly together a number of times, and a
somewhat similar sound will be produced, which will
show how much the *air* has to do with the case.

The food of the partridge consists of berries,
seeds, buds, catkins, insects, and wild fruit.   In the
autumn he will occasionally visit the orchard, and I
have often discovered him beneath some wild apple
tree in a copse by the river picking at the fallen fruit.
In winter the bird still finds ample nourishment
in the wild woods of the northern mountains, and
what with wintergreen (*Gaultheria procumbens*), his
own berry—partridge berry (*Mitchella repens*)
—creeping snowberry (*Chiogenes serpylli-
folia*), and an abundance of evergreen
leaves, he is far from starving; all
these he gets by scratching and
burrowing in the snow.   But it is
undoubtedly the case that many a
young bird perishes with its first experience of the winter's severe cold.

The partridge's
snowshoes.

In the Northern woods the par-
tridge will burrow to the interior of a snowdrift and
pass the nights of intense cold there.   The hardy

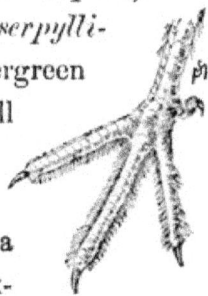

little creature is also provided with snowshoes, a curious fringe of stout, bristly growths arranged along the toes, which greatly assist him in walking over the snow. This growth begins to show itself on the foot by the middle of October, and by the end of March it has completely disappeared.

The flesh of the partridge, in my estimation, is incomparably superior to that of the quail, and the amount of it on the breast of a plump bird is surprising. A bird should be kept in the ice chest at least three days before it is eaten.

Partridge berry.

CHAPTER VII.

FURRY FRIENDS WITH FINE SKINS.

The Wolverene, Fisher, and Marten or Sable.

It is a question whether we are justified in considering the strange wolverene a furry *friend*. From one point of view he *is*, as his splendid coat furnishes us with one of the finest and most beautiful furs of the country. But he is certainly not a familiar creature among the northern woods in these days; long years ago he was practically extinct in the northeastern States.*

Dr. Clinton Hart Merriam writes that several were caught at Raquette Lake, in the Adirondacks, as late as 1842. Elliott Cones mentions the fact that a Dr. Z. Thomson, writing in 1853, states that the animal was then extremely rare in Vermont; and Mr. Allen asserts that as late as 1870 it still lingered among the Hoosac hills in Massachusetts. At the present

---

* His most southerly range is about latitude 42° for the eastern portion of the continent.

day all the skins which are brought into the market come from the far West and Northwest.

But we can not afford to pass the wolverene, or glutton, as he is sometimes called (*Gulo luscus*), with only a nod of recognition; he is entirely too interesting. His Latin name means "glutton," and his record in literature in this connection is quite unique.* He is the first and largest if not the most important member of the *Mustelidæ* family, that splendid furry tribe whose skins have such a high market value. He is also the most remarkable member of the subfamily *Mustelinæ*, which includes the long-bodied, short-legged martens, weasels, ferret, and mink. The skunk, badger, and otter are his more distant relatives, and it certainly would be inexcusably partial to consider these, and not the wolverene.

This strange animal is from two to three feet long —less than that, so far as general appearances go— with a chunky figure like that of a bear's cub. His coat is shaggy and blackish or dark brown, with light

---

* We find it gravely stated that this brute will feast upon the carcass of some large animal until his belly is swollen as tight as a drum, and then get rid of its burden by squeezing himself between two trees, in order that it may return to glut itself anew— an alleged climax of gluttony to which no four-footed beast attains, and for the parallel of which we must refer to some of the most noted gormandizers of the Roman Empire.—*Fur-bearing Animals. Elliott Coues.*

9

chestnut bands, which begin at either shoulder, extend down the flanks, and meet at the root of the tail; this is short, bushy, and characterized by long drooping hairs. His back is high and arched, and his head and tail are carried low. The forehead is a light gray color, and beneath the throat is another patch of the same pale tint. The head is broad and rounded, the muzzle pointed, the beadlike eyes are small, and the rounded ears (well furred on both sides) are set low, and scarcely extend beyond the fur in their vicinity. The feet are large and blackish, with sharp, curved, whitish claws about an inch long.

The wolverene, like others of its tribe, possesses anal glands which secrete a disgustingly nauseous, yellow-brown fluid, which is discharged by the usual nipplelike duct terminations situated just within the anus; the odor is ten times as bad as that of the skunk. But a more serious characteristic of this animal is his propensity to steal and hide things. He annoys the Northern trappers by upsetting their traps, stealing the bait, and sometimes killing and devouring the martens which are caught.

A Mr. Ross relates the following: " An instance occurred within my own knowledge in which a hunter and his family having left their lodge unguarded during their absence, on their return found it com-

THE WOLVERENE.

GULO LUSCUS.

"A strange animal with a chunky figure."

pletely gutted—the walls were there, but nothing else. Blankets, guns, kettles, axes, cans, knives, and all the other paraphernalia of a trapper's tent had vanished, and the tracks left by the beast showed who had been the thief. The family set to work, and by carefully following up all his paths, recovered, with some trifling exceptions, the whole of the lost property."

The most extraordinary habit of this strange animal is thus recounted by Elliott Coues: " We need not go beyond strict facts to be impressed with the wit of the beast, whom all concede to be ' as cunning as the very devil.' . . . It is said that if one only stands still, even in full view of an approaching carcajou" —the Indian name for the wolverene—" he will come within fifty or sixty yards, provided he be to the windward, before he takes alarm. . . . On these and similar occasions he has a singular habit, one not shared, so far as I am aware, by any other beast whatever: he sits on his haunches and shades his eyes with one of his fore paws, just as a human being would do in scrutinizing a distant object. The carcajou, then, in addition to his other and varied accomplishments, is a perfect skeptic, to use this word in its original signification. A skeptic, with the Greeks, was simply one who would shade his eyes to see more clearly.

The handsome fur of the wolverene brings a high

price among the furriers, the finest skins being valued at four dollars and the coarser ones at two dollars. It is said that the Indians and Esquimaux use the fur for fringing their garments, as they do that of the wolf, the skin being cut into strips for this purpose.

Another member of the *Mustelinæ* tribe, and one which approaches the long-bodied, short-legged form of the tribe more nearly than the wolverene, is the fisher, or Pennant's marten (*Mustela* * *pennanti*), often called the pecan, and rarely the black cat or black fox. There are two American species of marten which are distinguished apart by the following characteristics, according to Elliott Coues :

Mustela pennanti : Length, two feet or more ; tail, a foot or more ; ears low, wide and semicircular ; color blackish, lighter on fore upper parts and head ; darkest below ; no light throat patch.

Mustela americana : Length, less than two feet ; tail, less than a foot long and uniformly bushy ; ears high, subtriangular ; color brown, etc., not darker below than above ; usually a large yellowish or tawny throat patch.

---

* The name *mustela* means a kind of weasel. "Its adjective derivative, *mustelinus*, refers primarily to general weasellike qualities, and secondarily to the peculiar tawny color of most species of weasels in summer. For example, the tawny thrush of Wilson is called *Turdus mustelinus*."—*Elliott Coues.*

These species form the connecting link between the wolverene and the weasels, which is somewhat evidenced by a more heavily haired, stouter body than that of the sinuous weasel, and a slenderer figure than that of the wolverene. Of the two martens the fisher is by far the largest, as may be seen by Dr. Coues's description above ; indeed, according to Dr. Merriam, the average length of the animal is three feet and a half from nose to tip of tail.

The fisher.

The prey of the fisher is mostly mice, squirrels, partridges, small birds, frogs, fish, and sometimes hares and even raccoons. Strangely enough, he does not hesitate to attack the well-armored porcupine, which he kills by biting in the belly—so says Sir John Richardson. But I copy from Dr. Merriam's account of the animal the indubitable proofs of the fisher's liking for porcupine flesh, and whether he attacks the porcupine in a vulnerable spot or not, it is perfectly plain he does not have an easy time of it. " The intestine of one was lined with rows of porcu-

pine's quills arranged like papers of needles throughout its length, but they did not penetrate the sides.
Many were imbedded in the neck muscles, and in the
head, chest, back, and legs, but no inflammation was
caused. The needles were about two and a half
inches long."

The fisher is an inhabitant of the wilderness, and
in the northern woods he is occasionally seen prowling about the vicinity of lonesome ponds and evergreen swamps. Dr. Merriam states that the fisher
has been found of late years in the Adirondack
woods, and to my certain knowledge he still exists in
the secluded forests of northern New Hampshire and
Maine. Besides the few furs which come into the
market from the northeastern States, there are a
large number which come from the vicinity of Lake
Superior, Canada, the Northwest, and the Pacific
coast. The parallel of 35° is considered by Elliott
Coues the fisher's southern limit.

The name of the animal is somewhat misapplied,
as he does no fishing for himself unless it is on the
borders of the pond. On the whole the fisher is most
decidedly arboreal; he spends a great deal of his
time exploring the trees for his prey. He is agile
and muscular to a degree almost exceeding the athletic accomplishments of the cat tribe, and it is said
that he can make a descending bound of forty feet,

never failing at the end to secure his prey. He is, in fact, the expert climber of the family to which he belongs. In a race with the raccoon the latter's heels are not lively enough to save his hide; the poor coon has not a ghost of a chance. I copy what

"He spends a great deal of his time exploring the trees for his prey."

Mr. Peter Reid, of Washington County, New York, has said long years ago on that point: "While hunting early one winter I found the carcass of a freshly killed sheep, and by the tracks around it in the light snow perceived that a fisher had surprised a raccoon at the feast. A hard chase had ensued, the raccoon tacking at full speed to avoid his pursuer, the fisher outrunning and continually confronting his intended victim. I saw where at length the fisher had made an assault, and where a bloody contest had evidently ensued. The raccoon, worsted in the encounter, had again broken away and the chase was resumed, but with diminished energy on the part of the raccoon; the animal had been soon overtaken again, and a still more desperate encounter had taken place. The coon had failed fast, and it had at last become merely a running fight, when both animals had entered a swamp where it was impossible for me to trace them further; but I have no doubt the coon was killed."

It is said that the nest of the fisher is usually in a hollow, standing tree, from thirty to forty feet from the ground. The female bears from two to four young ones about the 1st of May.

The fisher's skin was evidently not very valuable when De Kay wrote, in 1842, thus: "The hunting season for the fisher, in the northern part of the State (New York), commences about the 10th of October and lasts to the middle of May, when the furs are not so valuable. The ordinary price is a dollar and a half per skin." Such a low figure as this would not hold good nowadays, for the least expensive Eastern skin of the *poorest quality* brings that price, and the most expensive one nine dollars. The average price of a good pelt is seven dollars and a half. Excepting that of the two otters, the fisher's fur is the most expensive of any belonging to the members of the *Mustelidæ* family. Its prevailing color is an admixture of brownish and grayish tints, gradually darkening into blackish brown at the hind quarters, tail, and legs. The real beauty of the skin lies in its rich, smoky brown tone.

American Sable.

The fur of the other, smaller marten, sometimes called the pine marten or American sable (*Mustela americana*), is almost as expensive as that of the larger species. It is by far the commoner fur of the two, and in many respects is quite as handsome. This smaller marten is one of the most beautiful of our little American animals, and is common yet among the evergreen forests of the North. His environment is properly the trackless mountain wilderness where the fir and the spruce cast their mingled shade over the tangled undergrowth of ferns, lycopodiums, shiny wintergreen, and gold thread, and the wild, troubled mountain stream bordered by lichen-painted rocks and gnarled, moss-covered roots. Here we may see his lithe, gliding body appear through the shadows, a bright bit of warm color set in the sober green of the forest. But the little animal is nocturnal in his habits, and one gets a glimpse of him only once in a lifetime; if it is early spring, one may chance to catch sight of the female in search of food for her young. Not infrequently she will be seen traversing the limbs of the trees hunting for the nests of the thrush and vireo. Martens are strictly arboreal in their habits, and they are not known to attack poultry. Their diet is usually mice in particular, and partridges, birds, eggs, frogs, and the larger insects in general; they are expert climbers, and go bird's-nesting with great success. As the whole group of *Mustelidæ* is characteristically carnivorous, I have grave doubts about this animal eating nuts and berries, as some writers aver.

I have said that it was a pretty little animal; at the same time I can not give a description of one individual which will do for all. There is such a great variety of color in the fur, due to season, age, and other conditions, that a single marten's appearance is no criterion for that of the genus. The particular animal which I remember best of all was tawny brown, not a reddish color like that of a fox, but a soft tone nearly like that of a lion, but darker. The feet and tail were darker, and the head lighter than the back. Mr. B. R. Ross describes the color of the marten thus: "In a large heap of skins which I have examined minutely there exists a great variety of shades darkening from the rarer yellowish white and bright orange into a variety of orange-browns considerably clouded with black on the back and belly, and exhibiting on the flanks and throat more of an orange tint. The legs and paws, as well as the top of the tail, are nearly pure black. The claws are white and sharp. The ears are invariably edged with a yellowish white, and the cheeks are generally of the same hue. The forehead is of a light brownish gray, darkening toward the nose, but in some specimens it is nearly as dark as the body. The yellowish marking under the throat (considered a specific distinction of the pine marten) is in some cases well defined and of an orange tint, while in others it is almost perfectly white. It also varies much in extent, reaching to the fore legs in some instances; in others consisting of merely a few spots, and in still others being entirely wanting."

The fur is variable, of course, according to season; in November it is in prime condition, and in winter it still continues full and soft, about an inch or so

deep, and with a great number of large black hairs
interspersed.

The pine marten is an agreeable little creature
when tamed, and is almost entirely without the unpleasant odor which is characteristic of the family to
which he belongs. But he has a pugnacious disposition, and quarrels with any part of the animal world
he rubs against. He fights and kills the weaker rodents, and is a terror to the woodland birds. He is a
sworn enemy of the red squirrel, as we may see by
the following account of Mr. G. S. Miller, Jr.: "At
Nipigon" [Ontario] "a trapper told me that the martens, wherever they occur in sufficient numbers, so
terrorize the red squirrels by constant persecutions
that the noisy rodents, learning that silence is their
best protection, stop chattering. Hence an abundance
of silent squirrels is, according to my informant at
least, a certain indication that marten fur is plentiful."

The little animal is somewhat shy, and retreats to
the seclusion of the deep woods upon the advancing
settlement of the country. I recollect that as early
as the year 1867 the marten was plentiful in the Adirondack woods. The early French settlers, in fact,
named one of the rivers having its rise in these
northern woods for him—the Ausable River. He is
still common in the evergreen woods of that region,

and hundreds are trapped there every year for their valuable fur. In Maine he is also common in the vicinity of Lake Umbagog, and he frequently appears in the spruce forests of northern New Hampshire. Notwithstanding his shyness, he is a bit inquisitive, and trappers say that if one should meet him and begin to whistle, his curiosity will overcome his prudence, and he will allow himself to be approached near enough to be easily shot. When he is trapped, if any one draws very near he will raise his hair, arch his back, show his teeth, and growl and hiss like a cat. If attacked by a dog, he will fasten on his nose if he can, and bite so severely that the distracted dog will frequently let go his game and suffer it to escape.

The female makes her nest in the hollow of a log, or rarely in some secluded spot on the ground, and bears from four to six young ones in early April. The animal when full grown is about the size of a cat, but slenderer and much shorter legged. The tail, hairs and all, is nearly a foot long, bushy, and in this respect quite the reverse of that of the pecan. The head is rather triangular and conical, and the eyes are set obliquely at the point where the muzzle begins to contract.

The finest marten furs come from the country north of Lake Superior, and from Labrador and

Alaska. These are quoted at from five to seven dollars each, while those coming from New York and New England rarely bring more than two dollars.

CHAPTER VIII.

FUR-CLAD FIGHTERS.

The Weasels.

WE may consider the weasels furry friends, if we look at the matter from an unprejudiced standpoint, and do the creatures the justice to admit that they are remarkably serviceable, not so much in the form of a muff or a collar as in the capacity of just and effective destroyers of vermin. If the wolverene is a friend on account of his fur, then the weasel is a better friend, because he can beat the record of the best-trained terrier in rat-killing. The sight of a weasel just issuing from a rat hole licking his chops after a good day's work, prompts one to call him a glorious fighter; the animal deserves our congratulations, and he gets them. But when he comes out of the henhouse and leaves thirty or forty bedraggled corpses behind him which are not rats, but chickens, then we reach for the gun and pay him in his own coin. In the latter case I should properly introduce him *hors de combat* and physically exhausted, as the

127

celebrated chicken-killer who has done his best! It altogether depends upon *what* he happens to have done whether we shall consider him as a friend or a foe.

Now, the next relatives of the martens are the little and larger weasels, the latter being the most bloodthirsty little rascal, taking size into consideration, of all animal creation. This seems a sweeping assertion, but I shall presently gather together sufficient data to establish the charge beyond refutation.

The little brown weasel (*Putorius* * *cicognani*— *Putorius vulgaris*, of Merriam) is a long-bodied animal scarcely larger than a rat. He lives along water courses, in swamps, and under rocky ledges, and his prey comprises a variety of small creatures, such as mice, moles, birds and their eggs, insects, and frogs. He is reputed to be an enemy of chickens, but there is no doubt whatever that some confusion exists between him and the larger weasel in the minds of the farmers. The latter is really the destroyer who enters the poultry yard, and *not* the little brown weasel.

The following are the principal points of distinction between the two species:

Little brown weasel (*Putorius cicognani*); length of body without tail, six to eight inches; tail short,

* From the Latin *putor*, a stench, in allusion to the putrid odor of some members of the genus.

cylindrical, black at the tip; color of under parts buff-white, sharply defined in nearly a straight line

Little brown Weasel.

beside the brown; feet white beneath; always turns white on the approach of winter.*

Larger weasel in his summer coat.

Larger weasel (*Putorius noveboracensis—Putorius erminea*, of Coues); length of body without tail, eight to eleven, or oftener nine to ten, inches; tail at all seasons bushy, conspicuously black-tipped for about one third of its total length. Color of under

---

* In Connecticut *P. cicognani* always turns white in winter, while *P. noveboracensis* never does.

parts buff-white irregularly defined against the brown; feet brown; turns white only in the northern part of its range. The male of this species is much larger than the female.

In respect to the general color both weasels are the same. But Elliott Coues makes an emphatic point of distinction between the two species, which is obvious in a comparison of the tails. He says: "This member is both absolutely and relatively shorter in the weasel than in the ermine. . . . In the weasel the tail is without the slightest bushy enlargement, and in most of the specimens I have seen there is no black whatever at the end of the tail; on the contrary, the end is frequently tipped with a few white hairs.* In other specimens, how-ever, the tail is dusky, while in one from Oregon the tip is quite blackish." He furthermore says, speaking of the skins which he had seen (from British America) of the whole animal, that "they were about six inches long, and also somewhat peculiar in the intensity of a liver-brown shade." Now Dr. Coues

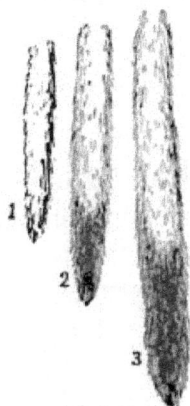

Weasels' tails.
1. *P. rixosus;*
2. *P. cicognani;*
3. *P. noviboracensis.*

---

* He evidently refers to the northern or Arctic species called the least weasel (*Putorius rixosus*), which is not found in the East.

has recorded the common color of the weasel as a variable mahogany brown, and he cites this peculiar liver color as an exception to the rule; but I must say that the weasels which I was fortunate enough to see last summer in broad daylight (at ten o'clock in the morning) were an unmistakable seal brown of a lightish tone, or liver brown—i. e., a color produced by mixing six parts sepia with one part crimson lake. But a mahogany-colored weasel I have never seen.

The weasel is an inquisitive little animal, ceaselessly active, and ever on the scent of his prey; this, it is said, he pursues with the intelligence of a hound. Mr. Thomas Bell describes the weasel's hunt as follows: "In pursuing a rat or a mouse it not only follows it as long as it remains within sight, but continues the chase after it has disappeared, with the head raised a little above the ground, fol-

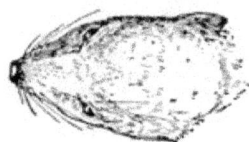

Head of little brown weasel, showing the narrow form adapted to the exploration of small animals' homes underground.

lowing the exact track recently taken by its destined prey. Should it lose the scent, it returns to the point where it was lost, and quarters the ground with great diligence till it has recovered it; thus, by dint of perseverance, it will ultimately hunt down a swifter and even a stronger animal than itself. But this is not all: in the pertinacity of its pursuit it will readily take the water, and swim with great ease after its prey."

The female weasel, a much smaller animal than the male, brings forth four, or more frequently five, young, and has two or three litters in a year. The nest is composed of leaves and herbage, and is warm and dry; usually it is built in a hole under some river bank or in the hollow of a tree.

As a rule the little brown weasel will most likely be seen in the woody borders of the meadow, not far from the river. Last June, during a most unprecedented flood of the Pemigewasset River, N. H., caused by violent rains, the weasels were driven from the river banks to the higher land at the foot of the hills. To my unspeakable surprise, I saw, one morning while weeding the garden bed in front of the house, a number of weasels traveling Indian file down the brick walk directly toward me. The baby (aged three) stood on the bricks, and as I handed him a bachelor's button in compliance with his request, I noticed that he seemed a trifle disturbed by something near his feet. No wonder! there were a number of long-necked, ratlike creatures plodding slowly along, within six inches of his toes, and grunting discomposedly like little pigs. On they came, the queer, dark-brown, bold-faced things, apparently with no thought except that the brick walk was the

proper thoroughfare to the gate, and that we were in
the way. I never saw so strange a sight. We stood
—the baby and I—within four
feet of the wide-open
rustic gate, which with
the surrounding coun-
try seemed entirely too
public to the weasels'
minds. I was still more
amazed, a moment later,
while three or four of the
animals were endeavoring
to insert themselves between
the boards of the plank walk
set scarcely an inch apart, just
beside the gate, to notice one
of the individuals return a few
feet, saucily stare us in the face,
and with a variety of hisses and
grunts show his disapproval of our
presence. Still another, much bothered by the publicity of the meeting,
took refuge beneath a neighboring sunflower, and, after squeaking and grunting
his dissatisfaction a moment longer, concluded to join his fellows under the plank walk.
After a while, with a good deal of scrambling and

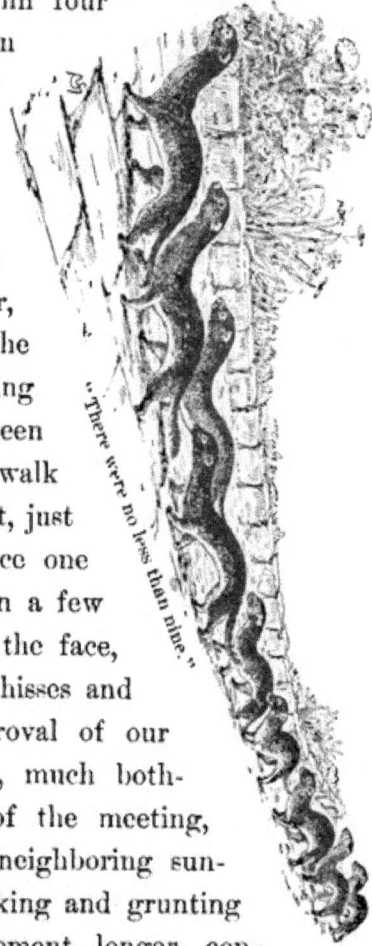

squeezing, they all succeeded in getting there. Then
the place looked deserted. But presently the regi-
ment reappeared—Indian file again—down by the
horse block on the road, at the foot of the terrace;
here I had a chance to count them as they marched
riverward across the road and disappeared in the
shrubbery on the other side—*there were no less than
nine.* I have not the remotest idea why so many of
them had congregated in the vicinity of the cottage,
unless the refuse tub around in the rear was the attraction. Truth to tell, on the borders of the wilderness more wild animals (and tame ones, too, for I
must include the itinerant cow) visit one's refuse
tub than may be found in a city menagerie!

I have often met the weasel, and he never impressed me with any shyness of disposition; but
others have had a contrary experience; for instance,
Dr. Abbott relates the following: " The careless
snapping of a twig may not startle you, but it tele-
graphs your whereabouts to creatures many a rod
away. . . . Not long since I was watching a weasel
as it tripped along the rough rails of an old worm
fence. It was intently engaged, following the trail
of a ground squirrel, perhaps. Suddenly, as if shot,
it stood in a half-erect posture, turned its head quickly from one side to the other, then rested one ear on
or very near the rail, as I thought; then reassumed a

semi-erect position, gave a quick, barklike cry, and disappeared. There was no mistaking the meaning of every movement. The animal had heard a suspicious sound, and recognizing it as fraught with danger, promptly sought safety.

"Extremely curious myself to learn what the weasel had heard—for I was sure it was the sound of an approaching object — I sat perfectly still awaiting coming events: the mystery was quickly solved—a man drew near!"

The assurance of the weasel, however, in the presence of his prey is unbounded. He throws himself on the unsuspecting victim like a panther, and

if it is a mouse or a squirrel gives it one bite on the head,

Weasel and a rat.

piercing the brain and thus killing the creature in an instant. His lithe, sinuous form enables him to bend himself in the most extraordinary way and seize his prey at the greatest possible advantage.

The weasel climbs trees with perfect ease, and rifles a bird's nest of its occupants or eggs, as the case may be. In the barn, among the grain stacks and hayricks, he is an invaluable friend to the farmer, for he will quickly rid the premises of all mice and rats.

According to Mr. Outram Bangs, the range of this weasel extends nearly across the continent, through the forest belt; his range has been positively fixed from Long Island and Connecticut northward to Labrador, and westward at least to Fort Snelling, Minn. He turns white in winter throughout this range; the hindquarters are tinged with sulphur yellow. The skin of this weasel has no especial market value.

The larger weasel, mistakenly called the ermine or stoat (*Putorius noveboracensis—Putorius erminea* of Coues), is not identical with the European species, which is considered so valuable for its white fur.* As a bloodthirsty character he has no parallel among the mammals; this seems to be a universal opinion among those who know the remarkable little crea-

---

* Elliott Coues, in Fur-bearing Animals, makes no distinction between the European ermine and this larger weasel. The differences, however, are very great, and more than sufficient to induce me to adopt the conclusions of later authors.

ture well, and there are apparently records enough
of his murderous deeds to amply justify such an
opinion.

One would never think, though, to see the pretty
little animal in confinement, that he was such a dis-
reputable character; but when I search among his
records I find substantially the same old story everywhere. Audubon, William Macgillivray (who describes the European ermine), Elliott Coues, John
Burroughs, Dr. Merriam, and J. A. Allen all tell
equal tales of the creature's relentless passion for destruction. Even E. P. Roe does not let him pass
without a just " dab " in Nature's Serial Story, and I
find the tale repeated there of his killing " fifty chickens in one night " out of " pure cussedness " has gone
the rounds of the creature's most recent biographers.
It is apparently unnecessary for me to add anything
of a like nature to these woeful tales, but I think I
shall be justified in telling one, the finale of which
will relieve the series from a character of monotony.
But first let us have some of that data about the
so-called ermine's bloodthirsty character which was
promised on a previous page.

Audubon says: " Yet, with all these external at-
tractions, this weasel is fierce and bloodthirsty, possessing an intuitive propensity to destroy every animal and bird within its reach, some of which—

such as the American rabbit, the ruffed grouse, and domestic fowl—are ten times its own size. It is a notorious and hated depredator of the poultry house, and we have known forty well-grown fowls " [later accounts make it fifty] "to have been killed in one night by a single ermine. Satiated with the blood of probably a single fowl, the rest, like the flock slaughtered by the wolf in the sheepfold, were destroyed in obedience to a law of Nature, an instinctive propensity to kill. . . . We have observed an ermine, after having captured a hare, . . . first behead it and then drag the body some twenty yards over the fresh fallen snow, beneath which it was concealed and the snow lightly pressed down over it."

Now let us hear what Elliott Coues has to say: "Swift and surefooted, he makes open chase and runs down his prey; . . . he assails it not only upon the ground, but under it, and on trees and in the water. Keen of scent, he tracks it and makes the fatal spring upon it unawares; lithe, and of extraordinary slenderness of body, he follows the smaller creatures through the intricacies of their hidden abodes, and kills them in their homes; and if he does not kill for the simple love of taking life, in gratification of superlative bloodthirstiness, he at any rate kills instinctively more than he can possibly require for his support. I know not where to find a parallel among the larger carnivora. . . . A glance at the physiognomy of the weasels would suffice to betray their character. The teeth are almost of the highest known raptorial" [preying] " character; the jaws are worked by enormous masses of muscles covering all the side of the skull. The forehead is low, and the nose is sharp; the eyes are small, penetrating, cunning, and glitter with an angry green light. There is something peculiar, moreover, in the way that

Face of a Western Weasel
(*Putorius nigripes*).

this fierce face surmounts a body extraordinarily wiry, lithe, and muscular. It ends a remarkably long and slender neck in such a way that it may be held at right angles with the axis of the latter. When the creature is glancing around, with the neck stretched up and flat, triangular head bent forward, swaying from one side to the other, we catch the likeness in a moment—it is the image of a serpent!" *

It seems as if this uncompromising, unqualified exposure of bad character was sufficiently convincing to go no further; but I must repeat what John Bur-

---

* Fur-bearing Animals.

roughs has said also. After telling of the manifold perils of a bird's life, he says :

"One day last summer my attention was arrested by the angry notes of a pair of brown thrashers that were flitting from bush to bush along an old stone row in a remote field. Presently I saw what it was that excited them—three large, red weasels or ermines coming along the stone wall and leisurely and half playfully exploring every tree that stood near it. They had probably robbed the thrashers. They would go up the trees with greatest ease and glide serpentlike out upon the main branches. When they descended the tree they were unable to come straight down like a squirrel, but went around it spirally. How boldly they thrust their heads out of the wall and eyed and sniffed me as I drew near—their round, thin ears, their prominent, glistening, beadlike eyes, and the curving, snakelike motions of the head and neck being very noticeable. They looked like blood-suckers and egg-suckers. They suggested something extremely remorseless and cruel. One could under-stand the alarm of rats when they discover one of these fearless, subtle, and circumventing creatures threading their holes. To flee must be like trying to escape death itself."

Very true, the rats are undoubtedly struck with mortal terror on the approach of this their deadliest

enemy.* But the rat makes some show of fight notwithstanding the desperate odds against him, and
sometimes he "turns the tables." Now for my story.

Not long ago, in a comfortable old farmhouse
familiar to me from childhood, but one much the
worse for the company of rats, a weasel appeared
around the kitchen way, evidently seeking for some
ingress to the partitions. At last he found the desired
rat-hole, and entered. In less time than it takes to tell
it, there was the dickens to pay inside the walls of the
old house; such desperate scrambling, rushing, squeaking, and shrieking were never heard there before!
Truly speaking—

> "You heard as if an army muttered;
> And the muttering grew to a grumbling;
> And the grumbling grew to a mighty rumbling;
> And out of the house the rats came tumbling."

There was grim death in the path of the destroyer for

---

* "We once placed a half-domesticated ermine in an outhouse
infested with rats, shutting up the holes on the outside to prevent
their escape. The little animal soon commenced his work of destruction; the squeaking of the rats was heard throughout the
day. In the evening it came out licking its mouth, and seemed
like a hound after a long chase, much fatigued. A board of the
floor was raised to enable us to ascertain the result of our experi-
ment, and an immense number of rats were observed, which, although they had been killed in different parts of the building,
had been dragged together, forming a compact heap. The ermine,
then, is of immense benefit to the farmer. We are of the opinion
that it has been over-hated and too indiscriminately persecuted."
—*Quadrupeds of North America, Audubon.*

a considerable space of time; then, in a tumultuous scramble, he reappeared in the kitchen in a desperate encounter with several rodents, and surprising as it may seem, exhausted and torn by the violence of the conflict. The rats were too many for him; he was worsted; and in two minutes more he was "as dead as a doornail," with a significant and appropriate surrounding of *disjecta membra*.

Dr. Merriam remarks that the weasel is ever victorious; but here is an instance of something quite the contrary, and although one's sympathies are not often enlisted on the rat's side, one can not help feeling like complimenting the old rodents which on this occasion broke the record.

The weasel, as a rule, does not eat the flesh of his victim when game is plenty; instead, he devours the brains, sucks the blood, and, when finished, goes for the next and the next victim, until, after a most terrific slaughter, he stops through sheer exhaustion. Relying on his strong, muscular jaws he springs upon his game, and "brains" it with a single bite. Hunting day and night, climbing trees with perfect ease, and entering the burrows of the rodents, he is a terror to all animal creation. Even the dog does not get the best of him without a tough tussle, for he will grab his nose if he gets a chance and hold on with the grip of a vise. Fortunately, he does not very often enter the chicken house; but when he does, it is good-by to the hens! In the field, or among the grain stacks, like the little brown weasel he is the best friend of the farmer, for mice, rats, and rabbits are his favorite game.

The range of this weasel is from southern Maine and Vermont South to North Carolina, and West to Indiana and Illinois.

In late summer, autumn, and winter the weasel's coat is remarkably beautiful. The change from dark brown in summer to white in winter is perhaps the most remarkable thing about the little animal. There is an irregular line of demarcation between the upper brown and the lower buff-white color in summer; this line begins at the mouth, and continues low down on the sides to the tail; all around the latter and over the paws is the same color as the back, but the tip of the tail is black.

According to Elliott Coues, the latitudes in which the change occurs in this country include the northern tier of States and the entire region northward. In this area, he says, the change is regular, complete, and universal; but, Audubon says, " in specimens received from Virginia the colors of the back had undergone no change in January."

Regarding the cause of the color change, about which there is much conflicting opinion, to those who, like myself, have observed the animal only in the North, it would seem as though Dr. Merriam's theory, recently expressed, is the one which is

correct.
My experi-
ence inclines
me to believe that
the change from
brown to white occurs
altogether too suddenly,   In his winter coat.   in many instances, to admit of any   other ex-
planation than that which Dr. Merriam gives, quoted
below.

Elliott Coues says: " As Mr. Bell contends, temperature * is the immediate controlling agent. This
is amply proved in the fact that the northern animals
always change; that in those from intermediate latitudes the change is incomplete, while those from far-

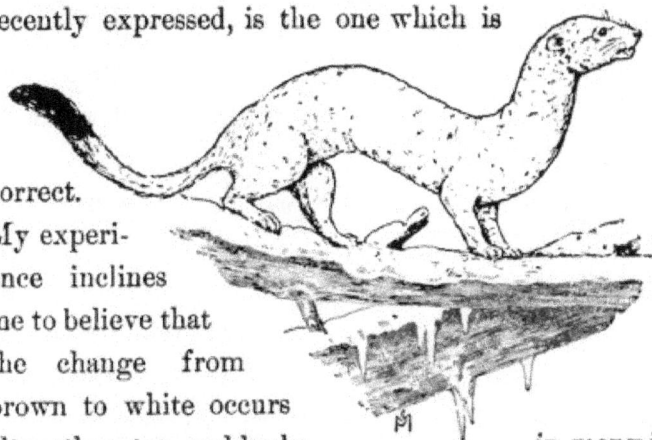

---

* We may safely conclude that if the requisite temperature is
experienced at the periods of renewal of the coat, the new hairs
will come out of the opposite color; if not, they will appear of
the same color and change afterward; that is, the change may or
may not be coincident with shedding. That it is ordinarily not
so coincident seems shown by the greater number of specimens in
which we observe white hairs brown tipped.—*Fur-Bearing Animals, page 123, E. Coues.*

ther south do not change at all. . . . The design or final cause of this remarkable alteration is evident in the screening of the animal from observation by assimilation of its color to that of its surroundings. It is shielded not only from its enemies, but from its prey as well."

Now I quote in substance what Dr. Merriam says to the contrary: "Temperature," he states, "time of change, and fact of change have little to do with the case. In the Adirondacks the ermine never turns white until after the first snow. In late October or early November, forty-eight hours after a snowstorm, regardless of temperature, the coat has assumed a pied appearance, often systematically marked and strikingly handsome; the change continues with great rapidity. By early spring the process is reversed; the change will even occur in a warm room indoors, although the transition is tardy; but it is really occasioned by the inevitable influence of hereditary habit."

In northern New Hampshire, among the great hills, the temperature frequently falls to 20°, and even 12°, between September 20th and November 10th. Yet, until the snow comes, the weasel remains brown. There is no lack of continued cold, either, between these dates, for almost every night in the latter part of October the mercury drops to the freezing point,

11

and frequently far below it. The larger weasel is by no means rare in this part of the country, and there is sufficient opportunity for a trapper to study his change of coat in early winter. The nest of the little animal will be found snugly tucked away in the hollow of some old stump, or in the sheltered nook between an old moss-covered log and a shelving rock. In early May the female bears from four to six young, which, it is said, remain in the vicinity of the nest all summer.

The white fur of the ermine seems to have gone out of fashion so completely that I can find no quotation of its value in the American list.

CHAPTER IX.

TWO FAMOUS SWIMMERS.

The Mink and Otter.

THE mink (*Putorius vison*) is the next relation of the weasel. Larger and heavier in figure, in some respects he resembles the marten; like this animal, he has a large bushy tail, but, *unlike* him, the ears are small and low, scarcely extending beyond the fur in the vicinity; they are rounded, and well furred on both sides. The feet are somewhat pointed and small, and the legs are short. Over the snow the tracks of the mink are mingled in one regular and rather deep furrow, quite different in this respect from the rhythmical tracks of the marten. On the sandy river beach the tracks are also a trifle mixed, and are easily recognized on this account.

The mink is a handsome animal, with a beautiful, long, very dark-brown or blackish fur, and black, bushy tail; beneath, his body is irregularly patched with white. He is tolerably abundant in the Adirondack woods; occasionally he is found on the borders

147

of the woodland lakes of northern New Hampshire, and rarely he is met with in the wilder parts of Massachusetts.

The prey of this thoroughly aquatic mammal, which, somewhat web-footed, swims and dives like a fish, consists of mice, rats, muskrats, birds, eggs, fish,

The Mink.

frogs, crayfish, and fresh-water mussels. He is, like the weasel, the particular enemy of the rat, who, it is said, gives no battle, but yields at once; the mink severs the main blood-vessels of the neck so skillfully that the deed is scarcely observable.* Occasionally the animal enters the henhouse or the poultry yard and makes away with a number of chickens and ducks; but, unlike the weasel, he does not proceed to wanton murder. He takes one chicken at a time, and most likely devours it, flesh, bones, and all; then, if he feels like it, he helps himself to another. When,

---

* Fur-bearing Animals. Elliott Coues.

THE MINK.

PUTORIUS VISOR.

" He even captures the speckled beauty
of the mountain stream."

however, food is plenty he is a bit wasteful. One winter a mink tunneled a passage under the snow to the troughs of the State Fish Hatchery, at Livermore Falls, N. H., where he captured and destroyed numberless trout, the remains of which were discovered, when the snow disappeared in the spring, in and about his nest. He is decidedly nocturnal in his habits, and consequently is not as often caught in his depredations on the poultry inclosure as the fox or the weasel; but he generally frequents the margins of rivers and lakes both night and day. The only one I ever saw in the wild state was busily occupied in the middle of a summer morning devouring either a mouse or a frog on the sandy border of a mountain lake. Dr. Merriam says he once saw three on the banks of the outlet of Seventh Lake (Adirondacks), and many times has met them in summer and winter about the water courses of northern New York. The little animal often prowls about the lakes of the Adirondack wilderness, he further says, and devours the remains of fish left on the shore near the camps. As a swimmer the mink is not excelled by any other similar small animal. He can remain a long time under water, and pursues fish by following them under logs and sheltering rocks. He even captures the speckled beauty of the mountain stream, for Audubon relates that he saw a mink catch a trout upward of a foot long. Exceedingly strong for so small an animal, and sagacious to a surprising degree, it is on record that he has dragged a mallard duck more than a mile to reach his hole and share the game with his mate. The writer * says: "As we followed the line we could easily trace the wide trail of the mallard as it was dragged bodily along over the fresh snow, and the deep penetration of its claws into the new ice spoke volumes of the force exerted by the small animal in the completion of so severe an undertaking."

When the mink is caught young, and tamed, he makes not only a good ratter but an interesting pet, although he resents any careless stepping on his feet or tail by using his sharp teeth with decisive effect. In his native wilds he is not a very timid animal, as may be inferred from the experience of Dr. Abbott.†

---

* An anonymous writer in Forest and Stream.

† "It was past noon, and rest was the order of the hour. What creatures I saw moved with great leisure, as if annoyed that they had to move at all. The mink crept along the prostrate log as though stiff in every joint, but when at the end of his short journey I whistled shrilly, with what animation he stood erect and stared in the direction of the sound! Half concealed as I was, the mink saw nothing to arouse his suspicions; he was merely curious or puzzled; he was thinking. . . . He did not move a muscle, but stared at me. Then I commenced whistling in a low tone, and the animal became more excited; he moved his head from side to side, as if in doubt, and needed but a slight demonstration on my part to convert this doubting into fear. I whistled more loudly, and moved my arms; in an instant the mink disappeared."—*Outings at Odd Times. C. C. Abbott.*

Elliott Coues describes the animal in its wild state, however, as being anything but amiable: "One who has not taken a mink in a steel trap* can scarcely form an idea of the terrible expression the animal's face assumes as the captor approaches. It has always struck me as the most nearly diabolical of anything in animal physiognomy. A sullen stare from the crouched, motionless form gives way to a new look of surprise and fear, accompanied with the most violent contortions of the body, with renewed champing of the iron till breathless, with heaving flanks and open mouth dribbling saliva, the animal settles again, and watches with a look of concentrated hatred mingled with impotent rage and frightful despair. The countenance of the mink—its broad, low head, short ears, small eyes, piggish snout, and formidable teeth—is always expressive of the lower and more brutal passions, all of which are intensified at such times. As may well be supposed, the creature must not be incautiously dealt with when in such a frame of mind."

Unfortunately, too, the mink has a pair of anal glands which secrete a fluid of disgustingly fetid and offensive odor, which is pretty sure to be emitted when the animal is trapped. Dr. Merriam says of it:

---

* When caught in a trap by the leg the mink is very apt to gnaw the member in a manner most painful to witness.

"It is the most execrable smell with which my nostrils have as yet been offended ; in some individuals it is only more powerful and offensive than it is in others."

According to my experience, the close-set, bristly fur is never without some remnant of the bad smell in spite of all proper precautions in curing it. In wet, winter weather, and in contact with the natural moisture and heat of one's neck, the "minky" smell is in strong evidence. To me the odor of the creature is far more unpleasant than that of the skunk ; yet Elliott Coues does not seem to think it is distressingly bad. He says : "No animal of this country, except the skunk, possesses so powerful, penetrating, and lasting an effluvium. . . . It belongs to the class of musky (!) odors, which in minute quantities are not disagreeable to most persons.

Of course, *de gustibus non disputandum ;* I candidly admit that I can not quite agree with Elliott Coues either with regard to the musky quality or the mild offensiveness of the perfume. Perhaps I experienced too much of it on a particular occasion long since.

The nest of the mink is made of dried leaves piled together about the thickness of an inch or more, and rounded in a snug hollow lined with fur and feathers. It is generally found in either a hollow log or a burrow. There are from four to six young produced in the latter part of April or early in May. But one litter is raised in a year. By nature the mink is not a good burrower, and often the female avails herself of the hole of a muskrat in which to build her nest.

Thirty years ago the fur began to increase steadily in value until the price of a single pelt reached five, and even ten, dollars. Dr. Merriam says he caught one whose skin sold for fourteen dollars; but to-day the highest price quoted for the dark Nova Scotia and Labrador skins is two dollars; those from New York and New England bring about a dollar and a half; and of the more southern and western furs, those from northern New Jersey to Wisconsin bring from a dollar and a quarter to thirty cents; and those from Ohio to Florida and Texas, from a dollar and twenty cents to twenty cents, according to color—the darkest fur bringing the most money.

Now the mink is the last member of the sub-family *Mustelinæ*, which is an important and large division of the general family *Mustelidæ*. The next subfamily is that of the skunks, *Mephitinæ*, only one member of which, the common skunk (*Mephitis mephitica*), is found northeast of the Mississippi, and consequently concerns us. But the skunk is so common and important an individual that, a little further on, I have devoted a whole chapter to his odoriferous majesty, and thus have taken him out of his proper position in the family just here. So for the present we will give the skunk a wide berth and pass on to his next relative; this is the badger (*Taxidea americana*), of the next subfamily *Melina*, another Western animal, whose eastern limit is Wisconsin and Iowa. It must not be inferred that this animal is one of the swimmers indicated in the heading of this chapter; he only happens to be sandwiched between the two swimmers by reason of his relationship. He is a burrower. But this incorrigible burrower, whose hole on the Western plains has broken more than one horse's leg and given more than one rider's scalp to the Indians, this miserable, broad-backed beast of secret and unknown habits, is too distinctively Western to command our attention; still, we will listen to a word about him from Elliott Coues, and then pass on. He says: "I have found badgers in countless numbers nearly throughout the region of the upper Missouri River and its tributaries. I do not see how they could well be more numerous anywhere. In some favorite stretches of sandy, sterile soil, their burrows are everywhere. . . . In ordinary journeying one has to keep a constant lookout lest his horse suddenly goes down under him, with a fore leg deep in a badger hole; and part of the training of a Western horse is to make him look out for and avoid these pitfalls."

Leaving the badger, we next come to the subfamily *Lutrinæ*, which is represented by the single
North American species of this genus, the otter.   He
is not very familiar through the well-settled parts of
the eastern country, but is still to be found in the wild
woods, on the borders of those charming lakes in the
wildernesses of northern New York, New Hampshire,
and Maine.

The beautiful otter (*Lutra canadensis*)—which is
a splendid swimmer and a great frequenter of mountain   streams   and lakes in the dense spruce
and hem-   lock forests of the North—
                              is yet reported from Lake
                              Umbagog, Maine, and
                              the lake regions
                              farther north-
                              east, the
                              lakes in

The Otter.

the Adirondack wilderness, the northern shore of
Lake Superior, and Bayfield, Wisconsin.   In the

South he is common in the wilds of Tennessee, North Carolina, and West Virginia.

The otter is amphibious in the largest sense of the word; he can remain under water as long as a loon, and can swim a quarter of a mile without reappearing at the surface. His prey generally consists of fish and crayfish, but he also has a taste for frogs, muskrats, wild duck, and poultry. He is an expert swimmer; he can overtake almost any fish, not excepting the trout, of which he is very fond, and in captivity he is partial to boiled beef. Dr. Merriam also says he is remarkably fond of crayfish (*Cambarus*), incredible quantities of which he destroys during the summer.

Otters are most restless creatures, traveling from lake to lake and river to river, and pursuing either a continuous or a devious course, "just as it happens." * They travel great distances in winter, and are with considerable difficulty overtaken by the hunter, so rapidly do they progress. They propel themselves over the slippery ice and snow with their hind legs, and, doubling the fore legs under, slide downhill and over snowy ridges in a most rapid and comical fashion. With the impetus gained by several rapid jumps on the ice they manage to cover the ground quicker than a swift runner on snowshoes.

---

* Animals of the Adirondacks. Dr. Clinton Hart Merriam. Transactions of the Linnæan Society, vol. i.

THE OTTER.

LUTRA CANADENSIS OR LUTRA HUDSONICA.

"The animal apparently enjoys a
regular sort of toboggan slide."

This remarkable propensity for sliding is one of the strangest habits of the otter. That the animal should apparently enjoy a regular sort of toboggan slide is almost past one's comprehension. But such is undoubtedly the case.

Audubon says: "The otters ascend the bank at a place suitable for their diversion, and sometimes where it is very steep, so that they are obliged to make quite an effort to gain the top. They slide down in rapid succession where there are many at a sliding place. On one occasion we were resting ourselves on the bank of Canoe Creek, a small stream near Henderson, which empties into the Ohio, when a pair of otters made their appearance, and, not observing our proximity, began to enjoy their sliding pastime. . . . We counted each one making twenty-two slides before we disturbed their sportive occupation."

"The borders of lakes and streams in the Adirondacks," says Dr. Merriam, "show numerous examples of their slides, and also wallowing places in which they play and roll. May's Lake, a small and secluded body of water abounding in trout, is fairly surrounded by them." *

The otter is an intelligent animal, of an easy and playful disposition that easily fits it for domestication.

* *Vide* Animals of the Adirondacks.

Audubon tells of otters which he had seen so perfectly tamed and trained that they never failed to come like dogs when whistled for, crawling slowly and with apparent humility toward their master. He also recites his own experience in taming several otters, which eventually he had the pleasure of romping with in his study. They were captured when quite young, and became as gentle as puppies in two or three days; they preferred milk and boiled Indian meal to fish or meat, and would not touch these last until they were several months old. The animals are not only easily tamed and domesticated, but it is said that they are taught to catch and bring home fish to their masters; they are taught to fetch and carry exactly as dogs are, and in the beginning a leather fish stuffed with wool is employed for the purpose; they are afterward exercised with a dead fish, and chastised if they disobey or attempt to tear it; finally they are sent into the water after a live one.*

The peculiar formation of the nose pad, about an inch long in full-grown otters, is the admirable means whereby the animal is enabled to dive and swim under water without inconvenience to the breathing organs. I

The Otter's nose pad.

---

* Bell's Quadrupeds.

quote what Elliott Coues says of it: "In general shape it is an equilateral pentagon, with one side inferior, horizontal, and straight across, and the other side on either hand irregular, owing to the shape of the nasal apertures, the two remaining sides coming together obliquely above to a median acute angle high above a line drawn across the tops of the nostrils. It somewhat resembles the ace of spades." In a word, this nose pad is a valve which closes over the nostrils and prevents the water from entering while the animal is diving or swimming. The otter in other respects is much like its congeners; the body is long and columnar, about two feet or more from the tip of

The Otter's webbed foot.

the nose to the root of the tail; the head is globose, the muzzle very obtuse, the eyes and ears are very small, the broad feet well furred and webbed, and the tail about a foot long and slightly flattened— i. e., elliptical in transverse section.

The nest of the otter is built under some shelving rock or uprooted tree, and sometimes in the hollow of an old stump. The young are brought forth about the middle of April, and there are usually two, or rarely three, in a litter. The mother and young generally remain together through the summer and autumn.

The skin of the otter is usually taken from the body without being opened lengthwise, and is in a prime condition in November.   The fur is seal brown, with beautiful lustrous long hairs, and thick, close under hairs of a rich but lighter hue.   It is the most valuable fur of the *Mustelidæ* family, excepting that of the sea otter, which in its prime condition brings from four to five hundred dollars for one skin.   The otter's skin is worth from three to ten dollars, according to color, the darkest fur bringing the most money.   The best skins come from Canada, New England, Lake Superior, and the Northwest.   Open skins have a decreased value of twenty per cent on the prices quoted.

CHAPTER X.

THAT FAMOUS ESSENCE PEDDLER,
The Skunk.

WHEN the twilight wanes, and trees, bushes, and fences become vaguely outlined in the gathering dusk, a strange little animal, somewhat resembling a black-and-white cat, ventures from his daytime hiding place, and we are aware of his presence in our immediate vicinity by a pungent and offensive odor. So, with bated breath and the suggestive whisper of "Skunk!" we quicken our footsteps and warily peer into the shadows on either hand; but alas for the luckless one who stumbles upon the little creature in the hasty effort to evade it! Nothing short of a Turkish bath and a complete change of clothing will ever enable him to regain his self-respect. He is an outcast from society, and, like the leper of old, must consider himself exiled from all the world.

The skunk (*Mephitis mephitica*),* another mem-

---

* The Latin name means a foul-smelling foul smeller.

ber of the *Mustelidæ* family, belonging to the group
Mephitinæ, is one of those few wild animals with
which no one is anxious to make even a "scraping
acquaintance." "Distance," I cautiously remarked

The Skunk.

one time to a skunk which appeared directly in my
path, "lends enchantment to the view; you may
have the right of way, and the path, too!" So I
gave him a wide berth, beat an ignominious retreat,
and breathed again when the atmosphere regained its
purity. One always feels secure at ten yards, but
within that distance, notwithstanding the fact that
competent authorities set the line of safety at *sixteen
and a half feet*, one is excusably nervous.

But, putting all prejudice aside, the skunk is not
only a much-abused animal, but one whose usefulness
can not be overestimated. Let us see what he feeds

upon : mice, salamanders, grasshoppers, beetles, larvæ, grubs, and caterpillars.* This is not a bad list, and, taking into consideration the fact that he makes away with a vast number of mice and grasshoppers, besides those insects which are peculiarly destructive to the hopvine, it is not surprising that the Legislature of the State of New York seriously considered a bill many years ago for his protection. Truth to tell, he eats more insects than any other mammal,† if we are to believe the testimony of at least three eminent naturalists, and it follows that he must be of great service to the farmer.

Some years ago I came to the conclusion, based upon a few observations, that the skunk was not only an interesting and useful animal, but a very beautiful one, so far as his coat was concerned, and that society in general, particularly drawing-room society, was not paying him the attention he deserved. To be sure, the skunk may not be an appropriate topic for the drawing-room, nevertheless his name is often whispered there, for the reason that his domain is now undoubtedly encroached upon by the outposts of refined civilization. The refuse tub of more than one

---

* I admit that he unfortunately robs the henroost at times.

† The excrement of the skunk consists almost wholly of the indigestible parts of insects, such as the black shells of beetles, legs of grasshoppers, etc.; it is remarkably black.

modern stately colonial residence has been visited by
him, and the evidence of his presence has wafted in
the open window of the parlor during a warm summer evening and changed the countenance of many
a stickler for propriety. Now, if the hostess should
remonstrate with the intrusive skunk, and the latter
could speak, he would undoubtedly reply with some
assurance, " If you do not like my neighborhood and
kind of perfumery you should not have located on
my territory; your drawing-room, like a weed, is a
thing out of place ! " The greater part of the country has always been the skunk's, and the site of one
of our great cities (Chicago)* was once his favorite
stamping ground. But, as I shall attempt to prove, he
deserves more attention and less evasion ; perhaps if
we knew more about him his character would grow
in our estimation, and we might cease to consider him
the " most disgusting thing in all creation." Interest
in so remarkable an animal, therefore, induced me to
search through his record and find some naturalist
who would know *all* about him. It must be confessed
that there is some difficulty in picking up knowledge
about an animal which one does not dare to approach
nearer than ten yards. To bridge over that ten yards
by another's experience, instead of pursuing investi-

---

* The Indian name Chicago means the place of the skunk.

gations at close range, would promise at least to be a method of procedure involving no expense in the matter of clothing.   At last I found a man who had at different times no less than *ten pet skunks*—one for each of my ten yards.   " Bravo !" I said ; " Dr. Clinton Hart Merriam has built the bridge.   Any man who has had the pluck to tame ten skunks undoubtedly knows the animal better than all the rest of the wise heads put together."   And so it proved.

But before we look at the skunk through the eyes of the scientist, we will steal a glance at him in broad daylight—a somewhat difficult thing to do, as he is nocturnal in his habits, sleeps all day, and is rarely seen before the sun goes down.   He is about as large as a small cat (I must not be taken too literally, for skunks greatly vary in size).   The head is small, the snout pointed—something like that of the European badger—and the long-clawed fore legs, which he uses to dig with, are disproportionately short.   In figure he is not a bit graceful, and his walk or hop is decidedly awkward.   His coat is black, long-haired, and with little or no white markings in some cases, while in others it is traced over the back with *two distinct white stripes*, which gradually merge into *one* at the neck.   The crown is usually white, and the forehead marked with a narrow white stripe.   His tail is large, bushy, long-haired, black, and terminates in a buff-white tuft.

He is the most deliberate little beast that ever prowled along the highway. A moonlit night is apparently his delight, and if we meet him then he is more easily recognized by his measured tread and cat-like figure than by his color. Even when frightened he does not break into much more than a hobbling gallop, and a horse at an easy trot would outstrip him.* Not infrequently he is run down in crossing a

The Skunk, showing the white marks on the forehead and flank.

road, and then—well, the country is perfumed within a circle a mile in circumference. As for the horse and wagon, they might as well be buried on the spot.

The skunk is not only slow, but remarkably curious. I observed one once, on a moonlit night, investigate a box trap which I had made for squirrels; he scanned it cautiously first on one side, then on the other, peeped inside, and sniffed along the edges in the same manner as a dog. At length, after appear-

---

* One night last summer one followed beside my horse at a slow trot for some distance without making himself disagreeable.

ing to meditate for a moment, he apparently came to the conclusion it was "no good," and marched off. Later on in the season, his visits to the cottage proving too numerous to be interesting, he was caught in a steel trap and shot—an ill-advised way, as I shall hereafter show, of disposing of him.   Dr. Merriam, in his admirable monograph on the skunk,* tells of one which peeped in the door of his museum, climbed up on the sill, scrutinized him with the keenest of black

Trapped.

eyes, and then began to stamp and scold saucily, finally backing out and into a beech tree near by, which so surprised him that he whirled about tail up, growled excitedly, and scampered off among the bushes.

The skunk makes frequent visits to the farmhouse, around by the kitchen way, but usually at seasons when insects, particularly grasshoppers and beetles, are scarce.   I never knew him to attack a rat, but I have seen frequent evidences of his destruction of field

* *Vide* Transactions of the Linnæan Society, vol. i.

mice and their nests. These he digs out with his long claws, and whole families go to make up his evening meal. He prowls around the wood pile, evidently after mice, and Dr. Abbott* relates an incident humorous enough to bear repetition here.

"The old wood pile was not infrequently the hiding place of one or more of these 'varmints,' which raided the henroost, kept the old dog in a fever of excitement, and baffled the trapping skill of the oldest 'hands' upon the farm. . . . With what glee do I recall an autumn evening years ago, when the unusually furious barking of the old mastiff brought the whole family to the door. In the dim twilight the dog could be seen dashing at and retreating from the wood pile, and at once the meaning of the hubbub was apparent: some creature had taken refuge there. A lantern was brought, and, as every man wished to be the hero of the hour, my aunt held the light. The wood pile was surrounded, every stick was quickly overturned, and finally a skunk was dislodged. Confused, or attracted by the light, . . . the 'varmint' made straightway for the ample skirts of the old lady, followed by the dog, and, in a second, skunk, dog, lady, and lantern were one indistinguishable mass! My aunt proved the heroine of the evening, nor did the

---

* Outings at Odd Times. Dr. C. C. Abbott.

men object. I often pause at the very spot, and fancy that 'the scent of the roses' doth 'hang round it still.'"

The home of the skunk is usually in some corner of the pasture, or perhaps on the shrubby border of the road sloping toward the streamlet on the meadow. Frequently he accepts a new clearing as a convenient home, and digs a hole for his nest under an old stump. The hole is small, cleanly cut, and is generally without the slightest odor—but that depends. Probably, if a large family—say, from six to nine members—remains in one domicile all winter, there is an appreciable odor in the vicinity. But it is a mistake to suppose the animal is not cleanly; the adults are very careful in the employment of their weapon of defense, and they do not use it except when they are in a dilemma. This is my conclusion, based upon considerable observation; and the fact that I have often met the strange little creature without having experienced any disastrous consequences, inclines me to believe that he is *not* aggressive. Give him a wide berth, and avoid a surprise or anything like a sudden movement, and he will not put himself on the defensive. Dr. Merriam is of the same opinion. He says that not one skunk in twenty will smell when caught in a steel trap, and that a person may drag both trap and skunk by the chain without danger if he proceeds very slowly and without making a sudden move; "but," he adds, "a young one squirts upon insufficient provocation"—a dubious fact which, to say the least, is disconcerting to the inexperienced, who can not be expected to "size up" a skunk in a jiffy and run if it should prove "ower young!"

The skunk is so common an animal all over the country that his unique method of defense is thereby proved to be quite as effective as any other means of protection common in animal life. I do not know of any animal that preys upon the skunk. Other creatures, however well provided with means of defense, find their match; even the porcupine, in spite of his quills, falls a prey to his arch enemy, the fisher; but all creation seems to "draw the line" at the skunk, and he lives a comparatively unmolested life. The miserable dog who has had an experience rolls himself in the grass or dirt, resorts to the pond, looks quite crestfallen for the rest of the day, and shows by an evasive eye that he has lost every atom of his self-respect.

Having perfect confidence in his means of defense, the skunk is perhaps the least timid of all the smaller animals except the weasels, whose audacity and calm assurance are simply unparalleled. But the skunk and weasel are not overconfident; there is everything to justify one's self-confidence when the world flees before one's presence. If we meet a skunk, we run; it is the hereditary habit of a skunk from the time he is born to feel sure we would run. Just so with the weasel: he is apparently born with the conscious- ness that the first rat he meets will shriek in terror and flee for his life. But the superior mind of man is more than the skunk can cope with; consequently the poor unsuspecting creature falls not only into every trap that is set for him, but into every trap set for another animal; and if there is anything exasper- ating about trapping, it is the discovery of a skunk in one's fox trap. Dr. Merriam relates how a number of these animals can be easily captured, somewhat thus: * " In winter the hunter treads down the snow from the entrance of the skunk's hole into a narrow path, and sets a number of steel traps at certain inter- vals along the route; at nightfall, when the mother comes out the young ones follow her lead, single file, down the path; the first trap near the hole catches number one; the others climb over the obstruction and move on until a second trap snaps on another; then the third trap catches still another, and so on until the whole family is taken in a single night."

---

* My quotations are not taken *verbatim*, because a slight con- densation here and there became necessary to save the limited amount of space at my command; but in each case I have rigidly adhered to every important point.

This seems rather stupid of the skunk, but it is simply the logical result of his dependence upon a special
means of defense; a trap is a machination of man
with which he can not reckon, but with man himself
he will reckon when he comes around for the trap.
In this respect his method of warfare is not unlike
that of the primitive Chinese, who threw among the
enemy vessels called "stink pots" filled with noxious
and suffocating fumes, which cleared the field quite as
effectively as shot and shell.

But now, for the scientific point of view regarding
this interesting animal, we must turn to Dr. Merriam.[*]
He had at different times ten live skunks in confinement, all quite young and consequently small—from
four to ten inches long. From some of these he removed the scent pouches, but the greater number
were left in a state of nature; these, he says, never
emitted any odor. A particularly clever skunk from
whom he had removed the scent pouches proved to be
a great pet, sleeping in his pocket while he was driving about on his professional duties, and walking close
at his heels when he took an occasional stroll after
supper. If he walked too fast, the little creature
would stop, scold, and stamp with his fore feet; if he
persisted in his rapid walk, he would turn about and

---

* *Vide* Transactions of the Linnæan Society, vol. i.

"A particularly clever skunk."

Photographed from nature by W. Lyman Underwood.

make off in the opposite direction; but if he stopped
and called him, he would return at an ambling pace
and soon catch up. Frequently the doctor walked to
a certain meadow where grasshoppers were plenty,
and there the little fellow would revel in his favorite
food. When the grasshoppers jumped he would jump
after them, and frequently he would have as many as
three in his mouth and two under his fore paws at a
time; in fact, he would often eat so many that his
distended stomach would drag on the ground. When
young, the courageous little creature would often
tackle a horned beetle, and he got many a nip in
consequence. When he caught a mouse he would
devour it all, and growl and stamp his feet if any one
came near while he was thus engaged. He was a
playful animal, and the doctor records a curious habit
that he had of clawing at his trousers for fun, and
then scampering off with the hope of a chase.

Regarding the skunk's most dreaded perfume, the
doctor gives us the following concise account: " His
chief weapon of defense lies in the secretion of a pair
of anal glands that lie on either side of the rectum
and are imbedded in a dense, gizzardlike mass of
muscle, which serves to compress them so forcibly
that the contained liquid may be ejected to the distance of from thirteen to sixteen and a half feet.
Each pouch is furnished with a single duct that leads

into a prominent nipplelike papilla that is capable of being protruded from the anus, and by means of which the direction of the jet is governed. The secretion is a clear fluid, amber or gold-yellow in color, has an intensely acid reaction, and in the evening is slightly luminous. On standing in a bottle, a flocculent whitish precipitate separates and falls to the bottom. The fluid sometimes shows a greenish cast, and it always possesses an odor that is characteristic and in some respects unique. Its all-pervading, penetrating, and lasting properties are too well known to require more than a passing comment. A well-closed house in winter became permeated by the scent within five minutes' time after a skunk had been killed at a distance of nearly twenty rods. The more humid the air is and the higher the temperature, the farther the scent is discernible and the longer it lasts. Under favorable conditions it is certainly distinctly recognizable at the distance of a mile. De Kay quotes a statement from the Medical Repository that a Dr. Wiley, of Block Island, distinctly perceived the smell of a skunk although the nearest land was twenty miles distant.

"The marked difference in the intensity of the scent in different skunks is chiefly due to the age of the particular animal from which it emanates. It is quite overpowering when there has been no discharge for some time and it seems to have become concentrated. When recently ejected the fumes are suffocatingly pungent, extremely irritating to the air passages, and, I have no doubt, are capable of producing œdema of the glottis, as are the fumes of strong ammonia; and when inhaled without a large admixture of atmosphere, the victim loses consciousness, breathing becomes stertorous, the temperature falls, the pulse slackens, and if the inhalation is prolonged the result doubtlessly proves fatal." *

Dr. Merriam does not consider the perfume of the skunk *one tenth* as disagreeable and disgustingly nauseating as the secretions from the corresponding glands of many other members of the *Mustelidæ*, particularly the weasel and mink. Nor do I. There is nothing putrid about the smell of the skunk; it is undoubtedly pungent and suffocating at times, but it is never sickening.

The skunk is a hibernating animal, but he does not sleep all winter long; during the greater part of

---

* There is a case on record where mischievous schoolboys forced one of their number to inhale from a two-ounce vial a large quantity of skunk perfume with somewhat serious consequences. The victim became unconscious, muscular relaxation followed, the temperature fell to 94°, the pulse to 65, and the extremities grew cold. The patient was unconscious for an hour, but finally recovered after the administration of hot pediluvia and stimulants.— *Vide Virginia Medical Monthly, vol. viii, No. 5, August, 1881.*

January and February he keeps in his hole, especially if the weather is severe; but upon the first appearance of a genuine thaw in March, just about maple-sugar time, he is abroad again. Dr. Merriam states that he has seen skunks scampering over the snow in midwinter when the mercury stood at 20°. He also says that they have large families—from six to ten young—all the members of which remain in the same hole until spring, but that not more than two adult skunks have ever been found in a hole at any one time.

It is not generally known, perhaps, that the fur of the skunk is quite long, thick, glossy black, and therefore valuable. The wholesale price of the finest skins, which come from New York, Pennsylvania, and Ohio, is from eighty-five to ninety cents each; the poorest, or fourth-grade skins, are worth only ten cents. The fur eventually "made up" goes by any other name than skunk—generally Alaska sable and black marten.

Of course thousands of the little animals are killed each year for the sake of their skins, and it is a fact, as Dr. Merriam explains, that no one knows how to kill them. His method is so simple and sure that I think it should be given a place here. "The skunk's back," he says, "must be broken by a smart blow from a heavy stick," and he adds: "If the animal is in a trap, approach cautiously and slowly; if you go too fast he

will elevate his tail, present his rear, and assume an
uncomfortably suspicious attitude. Give him a little
time, and he will about face and peer at you again
with his little, keen, black eyes. Now advance a little
nearer, be sure of your aim, and when you strike,
strike hard. The main thing is to keep cool and not
strike too soon. On receiving the blow his hinder
parts settle helplessly upon the ground, and the tail,
which was carried high over the back, now straightens
out behind, limp and powerless. As a rule, the head
soon droops and the skunk expires."

A heavy blow on the back given by a pole (not
too long), the doctor further explains, injures the
spine and thus produces paralysis, or a complete loss
of power in the muscles supplied by those nerves
which radiate from the spinal column just below its
point of injury. By shooting or decapitating the animal the ensuing death struggle inevitably brings
about a discharge of the scent. Audubon, however,
testifies to the contrary; nevertheless, my own experience teaches me that Dr. Merriam is right and Audubon is wrong. If there are those who wish to
satisfy themselves on this point, let them practice on
the skunk with a revolver, and escape the perfume if
possible. Also, it is not true that the animal limits
himself to one discharge; he is quite equal to several,
if there are sufficiently serious provocations.

13

There seems to be a universal and absurd theory that the skunk scatters the scent with his tail; this is an altogether mistaken and ridiculous notion scarcely worthy of passing comment, for it is evident that he elevates the tail not only from cleanly motives, but because it would seriously interfere with his aim.

There is one more fallacious idea connected with the skunk, and that is that his bite is attended by a species of rabies—*Rabies mephitica*,* as it has been called. This is all nonsense, and absurdly contrary to the "germ theory" of disease which meets universal acceptance among physicians to-day. A skunk bitten by a dog or any animal afflicted with rabies might transmit that disease again by his bite; but without such an occurrence the bite of the skunk will be a *bite*, and nothing more. It is true that his teeth are sharp and that they can inflict severe wounds, but nothing more unless he is diseased.

Probably there are few of us who could imagine the flesh of the skunk furnishing a dainty and choice dish for one's dinner; but, according to Dr. Merriam, it is far more delicate than the tenderest chicken. I quote what he has to say on the subject with the same

---

* This strange theory was not only exhaustively treated in an article in Forest and Stream (*vide* vol. xvi, No. 24, page 473) by the Rev. Mr. Hovey, but was seriously considered by Elliott Coues in a later writing; see his Fur-bearing Animals.

confidence in his judgment and admiration for his bravery that I have already expressed. He says : "I am able to speak on this point from ample personal experience, having eaten its flesh cooked in a variety of ways—boiled, broiled, roasted, fried, and fricasseed —and am prepared to assert that a more "toothsome bit" than a broiled skunk is hard to get, and rarely finds its way to the table of the epicure."

Hæc olim meminisse jurabit; but the next time we meet a skunk it will be just as well for us—now we have learned of his superior character but still lack that confidence which it ought to inspire—to deferentially step aside at least sixteen and a half feet!

CHAPTER XI.

THE KING OF THE WILDERNESS.
The Black Bear.

THE king of the wilderness, if the term has a reasonable application to any one of our wild animals, is undoubtedly the black bear (*Ursus americanus*). He

The Bear.

is a humorous creature withal, from a certain restricted point of view, and his dignity suffers in consequence. At the very mention of a bear we are inclined to be amused and interested, and it depends upon circumstances whether we smile or feel our hair stand on end. Most likely the latter happens when, without a rifle, we accidentally meet him in the wilds of the evergreen forest; here he is every inch a king, but, alas! an arrant coward—that is, under all ordinary conditions.

In captivity his humorous nature comes to the front. Not long ago, when I visited a certain wild animal "show," every beast, excepting those in the monkey cage, appeared to take life most seriously; but when I stood before two black bears all appearance of seriousness came to an end. Here a jolly couple were thumping about their narrow quarters, apparently trying to swallow each other crosswise, and evidently enjoying the sport

A jolly couple.

with as much gusto as college students do the rush in a game of football. Later on they subsided to the milder amusement of swallowing huge slices of bread;

but even this was done playfully, as though they didn't care a rap for such stuff.

But even in his native wilds the black bear is extremely interesting, and not without some irresistibly amusing traits of character, for if he should happen to visit the lumberman's camp while the latter is abroad, he will handle the jug of molasses he may find there with as much ease as a toper handles a jug of rum. Indeed, he is particularly partial to molasses and pork, and his visits to camp are far from rare.

The black bear is quite common in many of the wilder-nesses North

The Black Bear in the woods.

and South from Maine to Mississippi. He is yet frequently found in the evergreen forests of the White, Green, Adirondack, and Catskill Mountains. As recently as last summer, at a house not far from my cottage in the White Mountain region, I had the pleasure of feeding a young one in captivity with a pocketful of ginger snaps, which he took very

AT THE TWILIGHT HOUR,
MOUNT CHOCORUA, WHITE MOUNTAINS.

respectfully and carefully in his mouth, never offering to grab. Dr. Merriam states that in 1883 many bears dwelt in an evergreen forest in Lewis County, New York, twenty miles west of the border of the Adirondack wilderness; in the autumn they were in the habit of crossing the intervening valley and entering the Adirondack region, passing quite near the town of Leyden, his home. Here, within six miles of his residence, nine bears were killed in October, 1877.* Bears frequent the woods in the vicinity of Mount Chocorua, in the White Mountains, and they still haunt those giant peaks of the Sandwich range which overlook the pleasant valley of the Bearcamp Water.

During the winter of 1873 several bears were killed in the vicinity of the Twin Mountain House, White Mountains; and I recollect a young one, tame and intelligent, a great pet with the guests of the hotel in the succeeding summer, whose special delight was a bit of maple sugar or a slice of cake. Most of the afternoon he circumambulated about the heavy stake to which he was chained, and occasionally took a sitz bath in the tub provided for his comfort. One of his favorite performances was to balance himself crosswise on the edge of the tub with three paws,

---

* *Vide* Transactions of the Linnæan Society, vol. i. Animals of the Adirondacks. By Clinton Hart Merriam, M. D.

and claw a stick out of the water with the remaining one.

Of late years it is probable that extremely few bears have been found in the Catskill woods; but I remember as a boy a great sportsman's resort on the eastern slope of the hills not far from Cairo, called Barney Butts's, where bearskins and tame bears years ago were almost as common as chipmunks are now.

Caught in a trap.

One unfortunate young bruin which I remember better than the others had lost a paw in a steel trap; it was said that he had gnawed it off (a not uncommon thing for a trapped bear to do), escaped, and was recaptured after tracing his bloodstained tracks over the frozen snow. The limb eventually healed quite perfectly, and he managed by the following summer to do as well with three legs as most of his kind did with four. But I never could forget the picture which my imagination conjured up of poor bruin hobbling in anguish over the icy snow, a wretched victim of man's inhumanity; so he was regaled with cakes and lumps of sugar, the best way of showing him my boyish sympathy. The

last news I got of him in the fall was that he had
knocked the spigot out of a barrel of molasses somewhere in the neighborhood, and that particular part
of the country was very sticky.

Besides having a most extraordinarily sweet tooth,
bruin is decidedly omnivorous; his food is commonly
mice, turtles, frogs, fish, ants and their eggs, bees and
honey, wild cherries, blackberries, blueberries—in
fact, berries of every kind—fruits, vegetables, roots,
and not infrequently sheep, pigs, and poultry. If
you try him with a kitchen diet his taste is quite as
comprehensive; it includes cake, bread, muffins, pie
and pudding, butter and eggs, ham, hominy, sweet-
meats, crackers and milk, pork and beans, corncake,
gingerbread—in fact, excepting pickles, I doubt
whether he would refuse anything contained in the
larder. In his native wilds he will tear old stumps
to pieces to find ants and bees, dig out the nests of
white-faced hornets and yellow-jackets, and, caring
little for stings, devour the grubs with great relish;
scoop out the honeycomb from bees' nests, regardless
of the army of furious insects; tear down the branches
of the beech for the sweet beechnut; strip the black
cherry of its prussic-acid-flavored fruit (which is his
great delight), and clean out a blueberry patch of
every berry, ripe or green, without greatly disturbing
the foliage. Besides the huckleberry, the beautiful

china-white snowberry, and the common wintergreen
(*Gaultheria procumbens*), to all of which the bear is
partial, there is another mountain berry actually
named for him, the bearberry (*Arctostaphylos Ura-*

Bearberry.

Ursi), of which he is said to be
particularly fond. But he does
not always confine himself to
the wilderness in his search for
sustenance: he is a great rover,
especially in autumn, and not
infrequently he comes down
the mountain side and plun-
ders the orchard of its fruit;

he will even enter the barnyard, and his presence
there is the immediate signal for an uproarious commotion among the animals. It is a great pity one
can not persuade the horse that the bear is quite as
much of a coward as himself. Indeed, two such cow-
ards it would be difficult to find the like of throughout the animal kingdom. I have rarely heard of a
black bear attacking any creature larger than a calf,
and in the presence of a bear a horse loses his head,
shies, jumps, trembles like an aspen, and bolts if he
gets a chance. For that matter, the keen-scented horse
will smell a bear through a two-inch pine board, and
the intervening side of a barn is, of course, far from
reassuring to him. Last summer an itinerant French-

man, with a performing bear—a remarkably large
and handsome one, of the cinnamon species—stopped
before my mountain home one warm day and put the
great hulking creature through a variety of performances, to the infinite delight of the children.   He was
the best of bears, good-natured—if ever there was one
that could be called so—and exceedingly mild-eyed;
he ate the cold muffins we gave him with a "that's-
not-half-bad" expression, and hugged the pail of water as though it were a gift never to be parted with;
yet, after he had gone as peacefully as he had come,
he innocently spread terror among the horses he
passed along the highway just above, near the Profile
House; and not long after I heard that our friend
the Frenchman was in durance vile as a disturber of
the peace—of horses!

Now, the black bear is as shrewd and cunning as
he is cowardly.   The hunter knows this, and has to
take the greatest precautions to get to the leeward of
him, and ultimately within rifle range.   Bruin is remarkably keen-scented, and the first whiff he gets of
"a man in the air" prompts him to take to his heels
at so rapid a pace that the college athlete would be no
match for him in a race through the forest.   I witnessed for an instant a fair exhibition of his running
power several years ago in Waterville, on the western
slope of one of the great southern ridges of the White

Mountains, named Sandwich Dome. It was the latter
part of September, and I was one of a small party
making the ascent of the mountain. We had come
suddenly upon the verge of a ravine, and there, less
than a hundred yards ahead of us, directly on the
path, was the huge
black form of bruin
beating a precipi-
tate retreat and
never favoring us
with so much as a
parting glance. There
was a moment's rustling

On the run through the snow.

and swaying of leaves, a
sharp crackling of twigs,
then nothing—his sylvan majesty had fled, and the
woods were as silent and deserted as if they had seen
no live thing since the birds sang in June. There
is a solemn silence in the forest, anyway, just before
the leaves begin to fall, but after that bear disappeared the stillness seemed dramatic, if not actually
oppressive.

Not many years ago a black bear was seen by a
sportsman while he was fishing in the east branch of
the Pemigewasset River in the White Mountain region. The great creature was standing on his hind
legs reaching for the ripe fruit of a black cherry; he

sniffed the air suspiciously after a few moments, and then made off in a direction opposite to that of the fisherman in the greatest haste.

In February, 1878, three Adirondack hunters while on a panther hunt came across prints in the snow of a large female bear; she was traced to her den, but was found already frozen in so she could not get out. After she was shot three cubs about three weeks old were taken from the den, but they were too young to raise, and soon died. In April of the same year another den was found in a swamp near Fourth Lake, Fulton Chain. The den, which was in the side of a knoll, was discovered by the proximity of the young cubs, who were playing outside and did not know enough to "go in" when the hunters appeared. The mother bear again could not get out, and was easily killed. In the following June a very young bear was shot by Dr. Bagg, also in the vicinity of Fourth Lake; it weighed about ten pounds,

Cubs.

and its stomach was filled with old beechnuts. The poor little creature had evidently lost its mother; and Dr. Bagg, hearing a strange squealing like that of a pig, imitated the sound with such success that

the lost cub came running toward him, but, alas! to
its death.

In the summer of 1882 the signal station camp of
the Adirondack Survey, in charge of Mr. Verplanck
Colvin, was visited by a bear in the absence of the
campers and turned topsy-turvy by the mischievous
brute; the tent was torn down, and blankets, books,
and instruments were strewn about in great disorder.
The footprints of bruin were found later, and Mr.
Colvin, catching sight of him, fired at and wounded
him, but did not succeed in effecting his capture.
Dr. Merriam states that the average number of bears
annually killed in the Adirondacks up to 1882 was
thirty or more.*   In the wildernesses of the White
Mountains scarcely a season passes without ten or
more being killed, and in the fastnesses of the great
forests of Maine the shooting of a dozen bears in
one season may be considered a mild amount of sport.
In the Red Rock district of New Brunswick in 1879
eighteen bears were killed, only two of which were
fully grown.   This part of the country is sparsely settled, and it is said that, through the depredations
of bears during the year mentioned, the farmers lost
more than seventy head of stock, which included even
horned cattle.

---

* *Vide* Transactions of the Linnæan Society.   Animals of
the Adirondacks.

BLACK BEAR.

URSUS AMERICANUS.

"A large black bear was seen standing on the verge of a precipice."

In the summer of 1881 the little propeller Ganou-
skie, which traveled through Lake George at that
time, while passing the mountain point known as An-
thony's Nose, ran down a large bear which was swimming across the lake (nearly a mile wide at this part),
and one of the passengers dispatched him with a
blow from an axe.

The bear, if he is in good condition, is an excellent swimmer, and a matter of a mile or so is no
arduous undertaking. When he is fat his specific
gravity is not much greater than that of water; therefore he can confine his efforts to propulsion. Several
years later than the occurrence just related, while the
steamer Horicon was passing the rocky ridge which
borders the lake at the foot of Black Mountain (at
that time burned bare by forest fires), a large black
bear was seen by the passengers standing on the
verge of a precipice; he immediately disappeared on
the nearer approach of the steamboat.

The time when bears den up for the winter depends entirely upon the mildness or severity of the
season; the long winter nap, however, is not profound. Bruin is not overparticular about the character of his retreat, provided it offers sufficient
shelter from wind and weather. A big hole scooped
out with his ponderous paws beneath some fallen
tree, a rocky cave on a mountain knoll, or even a

broad hollow stump—if it is big enough—is quite to
his mind. When he is ready to "turn in," his fur is
at its best, and it is then that the hunter prepares for
his big game. When bruin reappears—probably during the first warm days of March—he is not the
handsome beast that he was; a long fast and an un-
kempt coat make him look a bit the worse for wear,
so he is unmolested if he keeps clear of the farmyard.
Again, the time of his hibernation is almost entirely
dependent upon the condition of the food supply. If
food is scarce and the cold is severe, he retires about
the first of December; but if beechnuts are plenty
and the weather is mild he will prowl about all winter, and the female will den only before the period
of bringing forth her young. So long as the male
can find enough to eat he will not den, be the weather
never so severe. In the Yellowstone Park, which is
the largest game preserve in the world, the black
and grizzly bears are so tame and plentiful that
they have become quite a nuisance by their frequent
visits during winter to the garbage dumps in the
vicinity of the hotels on the reservation. Dr. Merriam states that it is perfectly evident bruin does
not den to escape either cold or snow, but to bridge
over that period when, if active, he would be unable
to procure sufficient food. The females also remain
out until the maternal instinct prompts them to seek

shelter for their prospective offspring, and in the Adirondacks they have been found traveling as late as the middle of January. Their dens do not amount to much, and are often hastily scooped out beneath the upturned roots of a fallen tree or a pile of logs; the nest is frequently made of bits of brush and dried leaves, without so much as a bit of moss to soften it. In severe weather, however, madam makes a much better bed, and frequently remains snowed under and walled up in it until April or May. The den is sometimes revealed by a small opening in the snow which has been melted by the animal's breath.

Mr. Frank J. Thomson has published an interesting account of baby bears born in the Zoölogical Garden at Cincinnati,* the substance of which I copy: "About the middle of January the female bear refused to come out of her den, and would not let her mate approach her; she was at once supplied with hay, which she used to make her nest comfortable and warm, and was then closed in. On January 26th the young were born, but they were not seen until the third day after, as she would not allow the keeper to enter the den; then, by feeding her with bread held high above her head, she sat upon her haunches and thus exposed her babies to view. Ap-

---

* *Vide* Forest and Stream for September 4, 1879, p. 605.

14

parently they were not more than six inches long,
dirty white in color, and quite hairless. After ten
days their coats began to show, first grayish and then
a variety of shades, which finally terminated in
brownish black. In forty days their eyes were open;
thirty-one days later they followed their mother to the
bars of the cage where she was fed; but she did not
approve of this, and led them back; the second time
they followed her she cuffed them back. After a
few more days she allowed them to wander at will, if
no one was immediately in front of the cage; but if
a visitor appeared they were promptly driven within
the den and kept there until the intruder disappeared.
As the young cubs grew older they climbed all over
the cage and had regular sparring bouts, ending
in a clinch and a rough-and-tumble fight, when the
mother would interfere and knock both completely
out of time."

The black bear has commonly from two to three
cubs, rarely four, and it is doubtful whether she has
more than one litter in two years. It would seem
very unlikely that the young cubs could fall a prey to
the fox, panther, or fisher, but such is the case; and
Mr. Charles C. Ward cites an instance * where an
Indian hunter, who knew of two litters of cubs which

---

* *Vide* The Century Magazine for March, 1882, p. 719.

he intended to capture as soon as they were old enough to be taken from their mother, was anticipated in one instance by a fisher and in the other by a fox. Of course the marauders entered the dens when mother bear was not at home, but out on the search for food; however, in the case of the fox, who was not sufficiently sagacious to time himself for his work, the bear arrived home sooner than was expected and tore the base intruder into shreds.

It is a surprising fact, not without pathetic interest, that the bear rears her young in late winter when food is so scarce that one wonders where the poor mother finds sufficient to keep herself alive.

Bruin suffers most at the hand of man, and is hunted to death in a greater variety of ways than I have space here to describe. When he can not be persuaded to leave his den by any other means, and he is inaccessible, a fire of moss and pine boughs is started at the entrance and he is smoked out; but he will frequently issue forth in great rage and trample the fire out. In a quaint old manuscript of Paul Dudley, dated 1718, there is an amusing description of a bear hunt, which I will quote in part: "Dog scents them & Barks. then they come out. But if snow be deep they wont stir: they then put fire in Hole of a Tree then the Bear will come

Thundering out whether they are asleep or only mope for they easily wake." *

On the whole, it is not to be regretted that the black bear is a good deal of a coward, for, on occasions when he is thoroughly aroused, there is usually some terrific execution with his sharp-clawed fore paws and

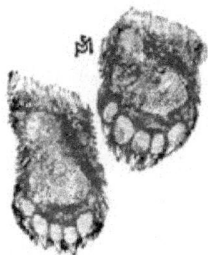

Fore paw and hind paw of the black bear, showing the plantigrade character.

his formidable canine teeth. A casual glance at his thick shoulders, however, reveals the true point of his strength; and his method of attack shows how completely he relies upon the big muscles of his forearm. He does not seize his prey with his teeth, but strikes a most terrible *downward blow* with his fore paw,

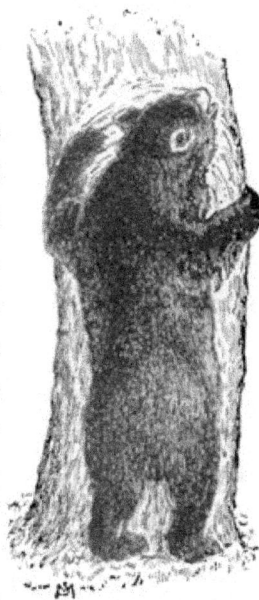

Bruin's autograph.

which tears flesh and bone asunder. The sharp claws are like steel hooks, and nothing can withstand the power which lies behind them. For some

---

* *Vide* Forest and Stream for December 26, 1878.

unexplained reason bruin exercises claws and teeth
on the bark of trees as he passes through the forest,
and thus leaves his autograph, which, sometimes to
his misfortune, serves as a guide for the hunter.
These tree marks have several times been noticed
in the wilderness which surrounds Slide Mountain
in the southern Catskills.   The bear rises on his
hind legs, and, embracing the trunk with his fore
legs, tears the bark with tooth and claw for several minutes, and then proceeds on his rambles.   Mr.
James Gordon, writing on Bear-Hunting in the
South,* records his guide's remarks on these bear
scratches (they are always made by the male) as
follows : " Look close, and you will see the tallest
marks are the freshest.   A young b'ar, feeling very
large all by himself, wrote his name thar fust.   The
way he does it, he places his back ag'in' the tree " (a
position which does not seem to correspond with that
described by Audubon †), " and, turning his head,
bites the bark as high as he can reach, which means,
in b'ar lingo, ' I'm boss of the woods : beware how
you trespass on my domains.'   The next b'ar that
comes along takes the same position and tries to out-
reach the first.   Now this old fellow has written in
bear hieroglyphics a foot higher, ' Mind your eye,

* *Vide* The Century Magazine for October, 1881.
† *Vide* Quadrupeds of North America.

young un, you're a very small potato ; *I'm* the boss that claims pre emption rights to these pastures.' Another reason for thinking it is a he-b'ar is that the shes have young about the third week in January, and it's about that time. We hunt them in February by examining the cypress trees, where they have left their marks climbing to their dens."

The black bear is a good climber, but he is too heavy to ascend into the tree tops. Often when hunted by dogs he takes to the tree, and then it is all up with him. A pack of dogs trained to hunt bears in the South is comprised of the most "or'nary-looking" curs, with pedigrees of confessedly vile mongrel strains. A few rough-haired terriers, active and plucky, to fight in front, some medium-sized dogs to fight on all sides, and a few large active curs to pinch bruin's hind quarters are all that are required to make a well-trained pack, which will only seize hold in a body when one of its number is caught; then it boldly charges to the rescue of the comrade, and, as soon as he is freed, it lets go and runs. Finally, gathering around the bear again, the dogs worry him until he climbs a tree.

If bruin is captured when he is very young he becomes quite tame, provided he is carefully and systematically trained ; but it is wisest to keep a sharp and vigilant eye on him, as he is not altogether trustworthy as a pet.* Mr. Ward confesses that his own efforts to tame young bears have not always been rewarded with perfect success, and he mildly writes that it is an unpleasant experience to return home from a journey and find the house surrounded by neighbors armed with pitchforks and muskets, the family shut up in the dining-room, and the pet bear, in a ferocious temper, having things all his own way. "Nevertheless," adds Mr. Ward, "if one is willing to endure that sort of thing, a vast amount of amusement can be got out of a tame bear."

The black bear is remarkable for its magnificent fur, which, when properly dressed, possesses great softness and luster combined with durability. At the close of autumn, when bruin has had plenty to eat, and he is sleek and fat with the rich mast gathered from the beech forest, he is jet-black excepting his muzzle, which is fawn color at the nose deepening to tan color near the eyes; over each eye there is a spot of tan brown. The profile of the black bear's face is characterized by a delicate convex line from nose to forehead; the

Bruin's profile.

* Read Bret Hart's charming story of Baby Sylvester, in the St. Nicholas for July, 1874, vol. i.

eyes are small, black, and intelligent, and the ears are somewhat rounded in outline; on the whole, his face is not an unkind one, and it has a certain canine suggestion both gentle and reassuring; but hunted down and in a desperate encounter with a hunter, bruin assumes an expression of countenance sinister in the extreme. Mr. W. W. Thomas describes a close and dangerous meeting with a wounded bear thus:* "I see the beast leaping on all fours, hind quarters high, fore shoulders low, head down and askew, snout turned to the right, lip curled up like a snarling dog, teeth chattering, and black eyes gleaming with a devilish light. On comes the monster with his vibrating, grunting growl, Knar-r-r-r-r! As the gun swings up to my face I glance along the barrels, and see the snapping teeth of the leaping brute within four feet of my gun muzzle. I fire. The beast falls forward with a heavy thud at my feet!"

Bruin's voice is far from musical. After a queer sniff made by drawing in the breath there is a guttural growl, which sounds like a prolonged Gnar-r-r-r-r-r! far deeper-toned and more threatening than the warning growl of an angry mastiff. But in captivity the black bear rarely exhibits any symptoms of

* *Vide* A Week in a Dug-out, Harper's Magazine, vol. lxiii, 1881, p. 830.

a ferocious disposition, and his growls are few and
far between.   Not so when he is on the rampage in
the forest during the rutting season ; at that time he
scours the wilderness with a number of his fellows,
indulging in continual snarling and fighting.   The
collision of two such creatures in a regular up-and-
down fight is a sight which impels one to keep at a
respectful distance.   I recollect a certain bear fight
in a "Zoo," one time, which demoralized the whole
establishment for the space of several minutes ; during that time the earth trembled, and what with the
blood-curdling growls and thumping blows of the
hulking creatures, the rest of the animals concluded
the end of all things was at hand, and their cries were
proportionally energetic.

The flesh of the bear is quite good in flavor if the
animal happens to be in prime condition, otherwise it
is rather tough.   I can testify, however, to the unqualified excellence of bear steak taken from a young
and fat animal.

CHAPTER XII.

A MISCHIEVOUS NEIGHBOR.

The Raccoon.

A NEAR relative of the bear, and, like him possessing a humorous side to his character, abundant in all parts of the country, and constantly getting into mischief in his nightly visits to the barnyard and cornfield, the raccoon is one of those interesting wild animals whose appearance brings guns, traps, and dogs into immediate requisition; and the poor beast, hunted for his life, usually ends with his skin tacked on the barn door and his dismembered body in the pot. Alas for the coon! But he happens to furnish a very savory dish for the table, and he is reputed to rob the henroost; two excellent reasons for demanding his life—at least so argues the farmer.

Now the raccoon (*Procyon lotor* *) is by no means

---

* The name is significant: it is derived from προκυών (procyon), one who snarls like a dog; the specific *lotor*, Linnæus added, because the animal has a habit of dipping its food in water before eating.

THE RACCOON.

PROCYON LOTOR.

"He is abroad at all hours of the night,
and often on cloudy days."

Photographed from life by
W. Lyman Underwood.

an enemy to farming interests; what he may happen to steal in the way of corn and chickens is greatly overbalanced by the number of mice and insects which he destroys. His depredations are therefore insignificant compared with the havoc he makes among the homes of creatures injurious to the farm. Beetles, mice, and even rats, he hunts with ceaseless activity during all hours of the night, and it is impossible to estimate the extent of his services in this direction.

The Raccoon. But he is omnivorous, like the bear; he feeds on mice, rats, moles, turtles, toads, frogs, fish, insects, nuts, fruit,* corn, birds and their eggs, and sometimes poultry. He is abroad at all hours of the night, and often on cloudy days.

There is no question about the abundance of life

---

* Dr. Abbott tells of a coon he once saw in a tree whose mouth was apparently reeking with gore, but upon a closer view of the animal and his environment he found that he had been indulging his taste for wild grapes. The tree was draped with the vines, and the coon had liberally helped himself to the ripe fruit, which had stained his jaws red.

in the woods and fields; there are evidences of it in every direction when we are strolling through the country highways and byways. It only needs a watchful eye to discern the unmistakable traces of creatures, both great and small, at our feet, within reach of our hands, and over our heads. I do not allude now to the ubiquitous toad, the occasional snake, the familiar squirrel, and the still more familiar sparrow : these are always in evidence. But the woodchuck's hole is not far off, if we will look for it the salamander's tracks are traced in the sand around every other stone on the margin of the brook, the marks of the porcupine's teeth are on the corner of the woodshed, the tattooing of the sap sucker decorates the trunk of the apple tree, the weasel's home is under the decaying log, the fox leaves feathers and bony relics at the threshold of his burrow, the raccoon leaves his footprints in the muddy margin of the pond, the turtle trails a curious pattern on the sandy shore of the river, and strange paws mark the black mud around the spring in the mountain forest.

Not only are the homes and haunts of many familiar creatures around about us, but also the evidences of many a tragedy. Here, just under the bushes beside the road, is a dead chipmunk; a glance at the place where his head ought to be is sufficient to identify the murderer; he was undoubtedly a weasel. There are some spots of red on the clover beside a tiny hole in the meadow grass; here was the home of a field mouse who was captured last night, perhaps by a coon. There is the daintiest kind of a footprint in the soft earth near by; it is like a miniature hand pressed lightly on the ground; whose is it? Look at a coon's fore paw and the question is answered.

The Coon's paw.

In the coon we have another animal which, like the cat, loves to be out by the light of the moon. If we desire to meet this nocturnal prowler, we must prowl also up to a late hour at night. Of course it will be good luck if we catch a single glimpse of him after prowling about through outrageously late hours during every night throughout the summer! Notwithstanding we see evidences of his presence in the vicinity, he does not appear; but set a

The moonlight prowler.

trap with a chicken leg or a bit of toasted codfish, and ·there he is the next morning, poor frightened

Coon's face.

beast, with a sinister expression on his pretty face. There is nothing in all Nature so striking as the black setting of his eyes with the surrounding ring of white. There is an appealing look in the creature's face, despite his threatening aspect. Who is cold-blooded enough to kill him?

Coon-hunting in the South, however, by moonlight, seems to be a regular institution. When the corn is ripe in September, " Marse Coon " steps into the field as the shades of evening have deepened and helps himself to a few choice ears, stripping them of their husks with his dainty fore paws quite as well as a pretty girl with deft fingers does at a corn-husking. He is very fond of the succulent, milky kernels, and very handy with his paws ; but, alas! he is so preoccupied with his feasting that the wretched dogs are soon upon his scent, and close upon his heels

Coon eating corn.

before he has realized his danger. He runs for his life, but one of the dogs is at him, and in an instant

" Out of harm's way,
treed."

Photographed from life by
W. Lyman Underwood.

there is a snarling scuffle, too vaguely outlined in the light of the moon to enable one to determine the issue; but the dog evidently knows more about coons' teeth than to his liking, and Marse Coon escapes. Again other dogs catch up, and there is a big scrap this time just under a gum tree; but by some quick work with his teeth the coon procures a stay of proceedings, in the midst of which he makes a dart like lightning for the trunk of the tree and gains it without another encounter. Up he goes spirally, and soon is lodged in a crotch out of harm's way—"treed." There is instantly more bark — dogs' bark — around that tree than ever was known before in all its history! The coon was more than a match for the dogs. But along comes the hunter with his gun; and who, however brave, is a match for the gun?

The coon is a fair climber, as a glance at his claws will amply testify; but he is no match in tree-climbing for the members of the *Mustelidæ* family—the martens and the weasels—nor for the red squirrel. Indeed, he is not arboreal, in the strict sense of the term, and I very much doubt whether he can be included among the enemies of the birds without positive injustice to his character. He does not pursue his prey among the tree tops, and is rarely seen in a tree above some crotch in the lower branches. His home, it is true, may be well up in the hollow of a dead limb, but his hunting expeditions are mostly made on *terra firma*.

Remarkably bright and winning in manners when tamed, the coon enjoys special privileges as a pet. He is frequently given the freedom of the house, as he never attempts to run away; but the consequences of his freedom are sometimes disastrous to the house-keeper. He is the very soul of mischief, and his curiosity has no bounds; nothing within reach is safe from his meddlesome fingers, and woe unto the kitchen pantry which he enters! Like his cousin the black bear, he is especially fond of "sweets." Mo-lasses, sugar, preserves, and cake—everything, he samples them all with infinite satisfaction, and scatters the remains of his feast with a noble disregard for consequences. Sugar, milk, lard, butter, and broken eggs cover the shelves and mix together in such generous quantities that only the hot oven is needed to convert the mess into some nameless kind of cake! It is not an agreeable sight for the house-keeper to enter the pantry and surprise the pet coon seated in the sugar barrel and oozing molasses at the tip of every hair.

But I do not exaggerate: he is on record as having done all these things. It does not make much differ-ence where he is, his propensity for mischief finds a sufficient means for exercise. The last coon I made the acquaintance of was chained to keep him out of trouble. He was the pet of the proprietor of a tobacco shop, and before he was chained he took it into his head, one Sunday, to sample the cigars. "My stars!" said the salesman who told me of the incident, "you just oughter 'uv seen this shop o' Monday mornin'! Sech a sight! Boxes o' Henry Clays upsot over the floor; the best Havanas all chawed up and spit out—not one or two, but scores o' 'em; tobacky jars knocked down and smashed; 'Dill's best' all dragged outen de boxes, an' de best Carolina mixed sprinkled over the floor like sawdust; and when I looked aroun', there sot that coon in the corner lickin' his chops kinder apologizin' like, and seemin' to say, 'I had a d——l of a time yesterday, young feller, tryin' to find somethin' fit to eat'. An' I reckon *I'd* a worse time that day clearin' up. Since then we kep 'im chained. He's young, but he ain't no fool, and he's beggin' now for a lump o' sugar—here, you young rascal!"—and he gave him one. While my informant talked the coon dodged his head about, turned a few somersaults, clawed at the man's trousers, and by other unmistakable means showed that he would relish some kind of a tidbit not in the line of tobacco.

I made several sketches of him on the spot, the results of which appear in these pages. Most of the

15

day he seemed to sleep, coiled up in a corner, but about four o'clock he roused himself and solicited a little attention.

The coon's voice is not a musical one; he has a sharp, snarling cry, not very loud, and a discordant, growling Gnar-r-r-r! when he is angered; but on the whole he is a good-natured beast, who likes company whether he is in the wild state or domesticated. It is rarely the case that a coon chooses to live in a particular part of the country

Coon asleep in the willows.

try quite alone; he goes in company on his foraging expeditions, and it is said that several members of a single family will live together in amity and make their excursions together, leaving the nest for several days at a time.

The female bears from four to six young about the middle of April, and these stay with the mother throughout the year. They hibernate during the severe part of the winter, and reappear, according to

"On the whole he is a good-natured beast."
Photographed from life by W. Lyman Underwood.

the abatement of the cold, from February to March.
Truth to tell, the coon does not fancy cooling his heels
in the snow any more than comfort-loving puss; and
the retirement of the chimney corner, in his state of
domesticity, is far more to his taste.   But his hereditary habits are such that when he stirs himself into
activity, about five in the afternoon, it is wise to keep
the pantry door closed, or he will make a night of
it.   There are records of his having drawn corks
from bottles, removed the covers from butter tubs,
lifted latches, and even turned door knobs.

So clever an animal ought not to be so easily
trapped; yet he is.   I recollect two summers ago
that my neighbor and right-hand man, the esteemed
guardian of my mountain home, remarked one day
that a coon had appeared the night before in his
dooryard.   "I'll have him to-morrow," he added;
and he did.   The trap was set that night, and the
unsuspicious coon made the fatal error of trusting too
much in the harmlessness of things in general and
man in particular.   We both of us had coon stew for
dinner shortly afterward, and the pelt of the poor
trusting creature decorated the barn door, as might
be expected.

The flesh of a young coon is tender and delicately
flavored, if it is properly cooked; but, as in the case
of any other animal, it is tough and unsavory if the

creature is old. On the whole, between young rabbit, coon, frog's legs, and chicken, each "done to a turn," give me the chicken last. It is a great mistake to cook any meat whatever from an animal freshly killed; an interval of three days at least, and the temperature of a refrigerator, are absolutely requisite to bring flesh to the proper point of tenderness.

The fur of the coon is thick, long, and pepper-and-salt gray; the tail is strikingly ringed with black, and the face is strongly marked. Occasionally there are individuals caught which are nearly all black; the pelts of these bring as much as two dollars each. Coons from New York, New England, Ohio, Iowa, Michigan, and the Northwest have the finest fur, and these skins bring from twenty to eighty cents, accordding to quality. Skins from the Southern States and south Indiana and Illinois bring from fifteen to seventy cents.

CHAPTER XIII.

THE FARMER'S SLY NEIGHBOR.
The Red Fox.

HE is a much-abused creature, this red fox (*Vulpes pennsylvanicus*), and the reputation he has unfortunately acquired through his incursions on the hen-roost is not an enviable one in the animal world. But as a robber and a thief his deeds are not a circumstance compared with those of the weasel; the latter seems to delight in pure murder, without rhyme or reason, but the fox takes what he needs and leaves all else—to be sure, not without an eye for the immediate future, as one may frequently

A youthful Red Fox.

find him returning for a second or third tempting hen, and the relics surrounding his hole show that his

213

disposition is not an improvident one. On the whole, however, an impartial examination into his account with the henroost shows a surprisingly small percentage of loss to the latter through his subtractions. And again, I doubt very much whether the chickens which Reynard captures are taken from the poultry yard; a thrifty farmer with a well-ordered henroost is not bothered much by foxes. Reynard lurks on the outskirts of the farm and picks up, night and day, those lawless rovers which a slovenly fence invites to the freedom of a boundless world beyond.

No one but a farmer knows what a trial the roaming cow and hen are. If Reynard would only pluck up courage enough to worry the hind legs of wandering cattle and somehow or other head them for home, I am sure the farmer would gladly concede to him the itinerant hen. Without doubt the farm hand wastes more time hunting cows than listening to gossip in the country store. As for the roving and destructive hen, the expense of chicken-yard wire-fencing, and the depredations of half a dozen or more escaped fowls in the newly sowed garden beds—these are sufficiently exasperating to make one wish for a stray fox to administer condign punishment.

We can spare a few chickens for Reynard's sake; he will not take many, and he is so thoroughly interesting himself that he will amply repay us for the loss of a few bothersome hens, if we will take the trouble to study his marvelously sagacious character. He has little to depend upon in the struggle for existence beyond his wits; he is thoroughly carnivorous, and must catch what he can without risking a fight with creatures more fully equipped with means of defense than himself. Consequently his prey is comprised of only those animals which can make the least show of resistance. The skunk he will catch unawares, if he can; at most it will only be a conflict between sharp teeth, if Reynard can clinch with him before there is a chance for a bombardment. Then, among the rodents there are muskrats, woodchucks,

Fox asleep (showing the warmth and protection of the bushy tail).

hares, squirrels, and mice. Birds, poultry, and eggs he is, of course, especially addicted to; frogs, and even fish, he does not disdain, and I have known him to make away with the carcass of a horse in the winter season. It is even recorded by more than one authority that he is partial to wild grapes and strawberries; but I have no knowledge of his vegetarian proclivity, and I doubt whether fruit of any description would tempt him so long as there was a bird or a mouse to be found.

Our red fox is by no means the same animal as the English fox (*Vulpes vulpes*). The latter lacks the soft color of the former, the fur is harsher and not nearly so fine, the head is broader, the muzzle less pointed and shorter, and there is less black on the legs. I do not suppose, however, that the two animals differ very greatly in character, as the American fox is quite equal to his English cousin in an ability to hold his own on the very ground of his arch-enemy, man; and in this country, where fox-hunting has not yet become common, the fox needs all his clever wits to evade the cruel traps of the relentless trapper who means business and not sport. It is a fair fight, though, between the fox and the trapper; but the fox-hunter's childish sport offers the fox no chance; it is all rank injustice; he must run to his death and make a holiday for idle men and a pack of dogs.

In spite of his adversaries the sagacious fox still retains his place throughout the wilder parts of the country, and given some proper consideration he will continue to live without making serious inroads on the shiftless farmer's defenseless chicken roost. It is doubtful whether he ever gets a chance to rob a man of thrift. Our failure to recognize the common rights of life among the animals often blinds us to the fact that wild creatures are really beneficent servants in one way or an- other, and man is generally the one benefited. It is quite natural to picture the fox with a be- draggled hen in his mouth; but, as a matter of fact, he de- stroys a score of such creatures as rats, woodchucks, rabbits, and moles,

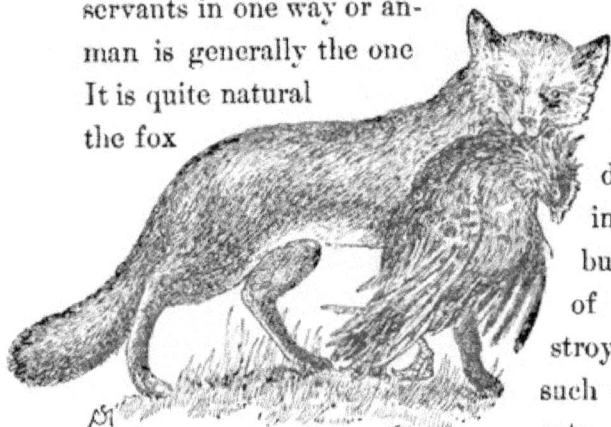

"With a bedraggled hen."

to every single hen. I know this by experience, for a casual examination of the vicinity of a fox's hole last summer revealed the truth beyond a doubt; but to be quite candid, I must admit that another fox's retreat revealed more chicken's feathers than would guarantee my proportion of one to twenty.

> "But all sorts of things and weather
>   Must be taken in together
>   To make up a year
>   And a sphere,"

and it happened that this particular fox took up his residence within a convenient distance of two shift-less-looking farms.

Not only are we apt to lose sight of the beneficent phase of wild life, but we are quite as prone to forget that it possesses any joy. We think the fox struggles for existence. What does he know about struggling for food and shelter? It is a joy to him to creep stealthily and noiselessly upon his victim, to gain his dinner by his wits, and to feel the satisfaction of an appeased hunger. A glimpse of a family of foxes reveals anything but the serious side of life. Nothing in the wide world is more attractively bright than the face of a young fox, and three or four of the little creatures at play are even jollier and prettier than as many kittens.

But when he is hunted by dogs the fox's struggle has begun in earnest, for it is a desperate and hopeless one. He leads the dog a chase over hill and dale to utter exhaustion, and at the end uses his needlelike teeth to no purpose; after facing each other for a brief space with panting jaws, the dog makes a lunge at the fox, seizes him by the throat, perhaps gives him one shake, and all is over.

When Reynard is trapped, a very moderate but sharp blow on the muzzle with a heavy stick finishes him with equal dispatch; at best one can not help feeling a bit remorseful after the deed is done, because it was so easily accomplished. But what a beauty he is! The ears and the long hairs of the

THE RED FOX.

VULPES PENNSYLVANICUS.

"A glimpse of a family of foxes."

tail are tipped with black; the fur is thick and
warm; the tone along the line of the back is a pale
burnt sienna; the tail is bushy and long, and the
gradation of color from the back to the stomach
through ruddy ocher to buff and cream is beautiful
beyond expression.

Reynard is not easily trapped, however; his keen
scent discovers the touch of a hand and the tracks of
a foot at once, and he will not approach a trap.   It
is often the case that the fox's aversion to water is the
means of his being entrapped by shrewd hunters.
The method of setting the trap is this: The bait is
placed conspicuously on a stone out in the shallow
water just beyond reach of the fox; halfway between this and the shore the set trap is sunken, and
over it is placed, slightly above water, a lump of turf;
the fox then, to avoid wetting his feet, steps on the
insecure turf, the trap snaps, and he is caught.

I do not know how common the red fox now is
over the country from East to West, but forty odd
years ago he was to be found almost anywhere.   Dr.
Abbott writes that in the vicinity of Trenton, N. J.,
the fox could be considered as extinct eight years ago,
although at that time he appeared together with the
wild-cat at long intervals.   But in the Pemigewasset and Merrimac valleys, New Hampshire, he is
certainly very common indeed; only last summer I

found the retreats of four wily individuals who lived within a radius of three miles in the valley first named. One of them visited a neighboring farm one morning very early, before the family appeared, and was seen complacently sitting in the middle of the road not far from the pet white cat. Puss did not seem in the least disconcerted by the strange visitor although he sat not ten yards away; undoubtedly he would have found his match in the cat if he had dared to attack her.

Reynard's proper environment is the hillside pasture that borders the wood; here he is seen—if one is lucky enough to catch a glimpse of him—at the best

In the hillside pasture.

advantage; his bushy tail, his splendid coat, and his vigilant eye are not eclipsed by the leafy undergrowth of the half-lit woods; and, what is best of all, one has a good chance to see his nimble legs beat a hasty retreat. There is nothing doglike in his ap-

pearance except it be his pointed ears; but even these
have a certain unmistakable foxy air about them, and
in a flash, when Reynard is gone, one's first impres-
sion that the strange creature was a dog is promptly
dismissed. No dog ever had a tail like that, nor was
there ever one so lithe and agile in his movements.
Reynard appears and reappears in and out among the
sweet fern with scarcely the rustle of a leaf or the
waving of a fern frond; that is his way. We could
trace any clumsy dog's course by the agitation he created among the leaves; but Reynard is accustomed
to steal noiselessly after his prey; the motion of a
fern might cost him his dinner.

In the morning and in the evening, in May and
in October, in summer and even in midwinter, we
can hear his short, sharp, nervous, rasping bark; so
strange is it that I scarcely know what to liken it to.
Perhaps it resembles the stridulous, rasping sneeze
of an old backwoodsman, or the harsh tones of a
parrot, uttered fortissimo. For the sake of a clearer
idea of the *kind* of a bark the fox makes, I may as
well show how it can be rendered by musical notes:

The setter dog has quite a different tone and, like all dogs,
he gives a series of short barks,
each one of which may be fairly represented by a
single note with an introductory grace note. The

fox's bark, however, is *one short, suddenly loud squall*, bearing not the remotest resemblance to the bark of a setter. The terrier's bark may be a great deal nearer in pitch, but it is quite as far off in quality of tone. Indeed, between the dog and the fox there is, after all, very little similitude.

Reynard's burrow is usually on the border of the wood, and perhaps beside some old stump ; not infrequently he resorts to safer retreats beneath the broken rocks which have fallen from the steep ledges of some mountain. He is a rather strong - smelling animal, and his home is consequently not without a characteristic odor, all the more apparent in the dampness of a summer evening. The female bears her young anywhere from the middle of March to the middle of April. She has from four

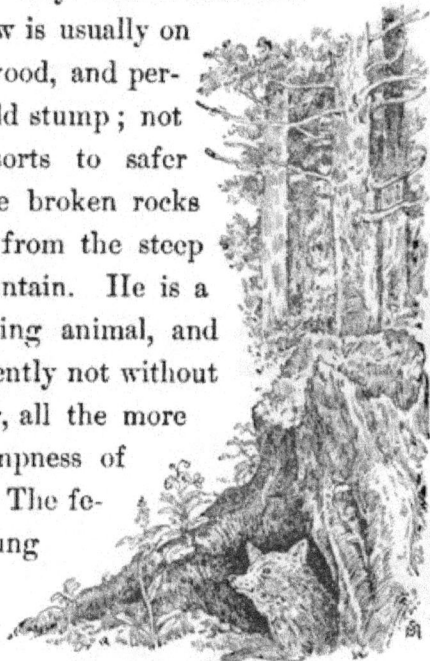

Reynard's burrow

to eight little ones, with the prettiest faces imaginable. They make famous pets when captured early in life, but unfortunately turn out treacherous and sly in the end.

The largest and finest red fox skins come from Canada, Labrador, Michigan, and Minnesota; these sell for a dollar and a half or a dollar and eighty-five cents, according to quality and size.

The gray fox (*Urocyon cinereo-argenteus*) is rarely if ever found in New England nowadays.* He

The Gray Fox.

is small, and it is said that he has been driven out by the larger red fox. But in the middle West he is still common from southern Michigan to western New York, and from northern Indiana to South Carolina and Tennessee. His coarse fur, which is stiff and long haired, is blackish mixed with silver-gray, behind and beneath the ears is a rusty tinge, and the upper part of the tail is very dark, characterized by long black hairs. The skin is worth about sixty-five cents.

---

* According to Prof. J. A. Allen, his most Northern range is not much beyond the parallel of 42°.

The so-called "silver" fox of the far West is valued for his remarkably beautiful skin, which brings no less than one hundred and twenty-five dollars if it is in its prime. The handsomest skins come from the extreme Northwest. But I must draw attention to the fact that there are but two species of foxes common in the country east of

Silver-gray Fox.

the Mississippi Valley: one is *Vulpes pennsylvanicus*, and the other is *Urocyon cinereo-argenteus*. The former species, usually called the common or red fox, is now considered the one species which must include the so-called "silver" fox (*Vulpes argentatus*), the so-called "cross" fox * (*Vulpes decussatus*), and the so-called Western fox (*Vulpes macrurus*).

The generally accepted opinion that the color of a fox decides the species, is thrown to the winds by

---

* The "cross" fox is more or less frequent as far south as northern New York and northern New England, and throughout the more elevated portions of the great Rocky Mountain plateau, where it constitutes a large proportion of the representatives of the so-called *Vulpes macrurus*. More rarely the black or so-called silver fox is met with in the same regions, becoming frequent in the higher parts of the Rocky Mountains and northward.—*J. A. Allen. Bulletin of the United States Geographical Survey, vol. ii, No. 4, Washington.*

Prof. J. A. Allen, who is an unquestionably high authority in the definition of species. Here is what he has to say about the common fox: " In the common fox we meet with a range of color variation irrespective of locality, somewhat akin to that seen in the wolf (*Canis lupus*). The prevalent tendency, however, is toward melanism,* which tendency is much more strongly developed in the colder than in the warmer latitudes. Frequently individuals of the melanistic type occur in litters of the common variety. The varying degrees of melanism occurring in this species have given rise to several commercial varieties, which have received at the hands of naturalists systematic designation, and have been regarded more or less commonly as valid species. Generally these melanistic varieties are more fully furred and have larger and heavier tails than the common form. The difference in the fineness and softness of the fur is recognized to such an extent by furriers as to greatly affect the price of the skins ; the so-called ' silver ' and ' cross ' furs being considered far more valuable than the fulvous type.

" With this tendency to great variability in color, we meet, as usual in such cases, a great variation in

---

* Melanism, or melanosis, from μελάνωσις, which means a becoming black.

16

size. In the present case the variation in color may be properly regarded as geographical through an increasing tendency to melanism northward. The variation in size is also chiefly of the same character, the size uniformly increasing toward the North. The largest specimens come from the Aleutian Islands and Alaska, and the smallest from Essex County, New York.

"The foxes of the colder regions, it is true, have a fuller and softer pelage, a greater tendency to melanism, shorter muzzles, and are larger; yet these differences are so inconstant—especially the differences of color—and so insensibly intergrade that any attempt at their subspecific recognition seems impracticable, the most diverse varieties in color occurring at the same localities and even among individuals of the same litter."

So it appears that the particular foxes called red, black, silver, and cross are all one species, with a commercial difference; that is all. But that difference expressed in dollars and cents is quite considerable. I find that the dearest red fox skin is quoted at a dollar and eighty-five cents, and the cheapest at fifty cents; the dearest "cross" skin at nine dollars, and the cheapest at seventy-five cents. The dark "silver" is quoted at from one hundred and twenty-five to ten dollars, and the pale at from fifty to five dollars.

The " cross " fox is so named because a dark band between the shoulders is crossed by another extending over the shoulders. The muzzle and under parts with the legs are black, and the remainder of the body is a tawny color.

CHAPTER XIV.

A FLEET-FOOTED NEIGHBOR IN THE WOODS.
The Virginia Deer.

To " run like a deer " means to run like the fleet-est-footed member of that highest division of animal

Head of a Deer about five
years old.

life in the world called *Mammalia.* Now the term *Mammalia* is a significant one with a world of meaning in it which few, perhaps, fully appreciate.* It means that the closest possible relationship exists between the mother and her young. And perhaps one of the most beautiful examples of a mother and her young among the animals is the soft-eyed deer and her dainty, snow-spotted fawn.

---

* The essential character of a creature belonging to the great group called *Mammalia* is that it is wholly dependent upon its

The Virginia deer (*Cariacus virginianus*) is not only the fleetest but the most sympathetically attractive animal of this great group. One who has once looked into the liquid eyes of a young fawn and its mother, and afterward has aimed a gun at one or the other with intent to destroy, following up the intent with its accomplishment, burdens his conscience with a sort of questionable guilt for the rest of his days. To slay such beautiful creatures seems something not far short of murder; but there is

Virginia Deer.

the venison to be considered, and as that is the meat of the epicure one's conscience must be smothered.

It would seem as if I stretched a point to include this rare animal in my list of familiar life; but I do not. Times have changed and the deer is not as rare as he was. Last summer there were many complaints

mother for nourishment during the helpless period of its infancy. The *Mammalia*, in a word, are animals which suckle their young; the term is derived from the Latin, *mamma*, meaning "the breast." Thus, we undoubtedly have sufficient reason to believe the endearing name *mamma* had its origin with the Latin word.

coming from the farmers in Vermont and New Hampshire because the animal had made some havoc in their cornfields. I do not know how much of an excuse such complaints were to secure a modification in the strict game laws of both States, but I suspect the average farmer was anxious to get a better chance at a deer. At present the laws are so comprehensive and effectual that the deer has a chance at

Two young Deer at El Fureidis.

the farmer! a fact of such slight consequence that I think we have no sufficient reason to regret it. Thrice, last summer, three deer made their appearance within a quarter of a mile of my hillside studio, and once two young ones appeared close by the pasture fence on the border of the wood, not more than fifty feet from the piazza rails. Repeatedly deer had been seen on the highway in the spring, and once one was chased on the track by a passing train.

In 1867 when, as a child, I was taken on a tour

through the Adirondack woods, there was not much choice of meat either at Paul Smith's, Bartlett's, or the guide's camp; it was pork or venison—which would we have? I need not say which we always chose, and as a consequence the bill of fare was like a delightful " theme with variations," thus: Breakfast, venison—roast, broiled, or fried. Dinner, venison—fried, broiled, or roast. Supper, *da capo*. Twenty years after, when I went over exactly the same extended route, I looked in vain for a sportsman with his antlered game; and at the table an elaborate menu, with a picture of a deer at the top, was handed to me to choose my dinner from—alas for the wilderness! it was no more. There was no such word as venison on the card.*

But of late years the game laws are beginning to bear fruit, and the deer is again on the increase in New York, Vermont, and New Hampshire. On what does he subsist in the snowbound forests of the North? How does he endure the cold? These are questions not so difficult to answer. As soon as the fall comes his hair grows twice as thick as it was in midsummer, so thick, in fact, that it helps to float

---

* Up to 1882 from five hundred to eight hundred deer were killed annually for the preceding ten years; that would make a fair estimated total of six thousand five hundred slain in this decade; no wonder venison was scarce in 1887!

him in water; by December it is like a door mat, but
not quite so coarse. He sheds his coat gradually
twice a year, in June and September, and it changes
in color from red-brown in summer

Lycopodium obscurum.

Lycopodium clavatum.

to gray in winter. For food he has young twigs—
those of the black birch he especially relishes—the
foliage of the arbor vitæ (*Thuja occidentalis*),* hemlock, and fir; digging through the snow with his

---

* The margins of some of the Adirondack lakes are thickly
overhung with the branches of the arbor vitæ; these are often
stripped off for a distance of five feet up the trunks of the trees,
the result of the feeding of deer which have wintered in the vicinity.

YOUNG DEER.

CARIACUS VIRGINIANUS, OR
ODOCOILEUS VIRGINIANUS.

"He works his way toward the
shore of the lake."

Photographed from nature by W. Lyman Underwood.

hoofs he feeds upon the wintergreen (*Gaultheria procumbens*), the lycopodiums, and many other green things, like mosses and lichens. Early in the spring he gradually works his way toward the shores of the lakes, and finds there pickerel weed, lily pads, and spatter-dock ; as the season advances he approaches the outskirts of civilization and crops the new meadow grasses near the farms ; he even ventures as far as the pasture bars, not infrequently feeding in company with

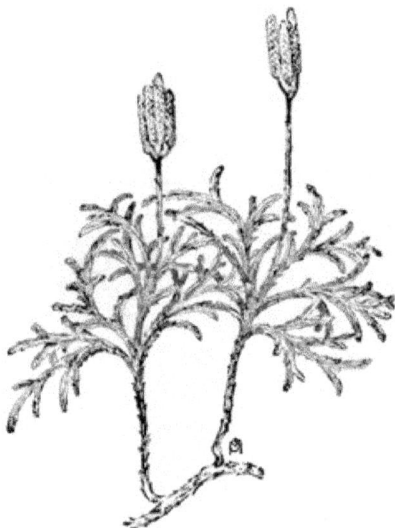

Lycopodium complanatum.

Pickerel Weed.

the cows ; but the latter are inclined to be suspicious of the strangers and sometimes move off to another part of the field.

From spring to autumn his food consists of numerous herbs, grasses, aquatic plants, leaves of shrubs and trees, and the berries of the mountain ash and dwarf cornel. When beech nuts are plenty—the trees bear in alternate years—these constitute a large portion of his fare. By the middle of September the

Bunchberry.

deer in the Adirondack region desert the water courses and retire to the more secluded parts of the forest.* Here they congregate during the deep snows of winter in what are called deer yards; these are certain sheltered localities where the heavy snow is trampled down and pathways lead in all directions toward promising food supplies, and where under thickets of spruce and fir the animals find sufficiently comfortable beds. Mr. Verplanck Colvin, speaking of one of these deer yards, describes it as resembling a sheep yard in winter.†

The deer is not a strictly nocturnal animal, although he haunts the shores of the Adirondack lakes

---

* *Vide* Transactions of the Linnæan Society. Animals of the Adirondacks. Dr. C. H. Merriam.

† *Vide* Report of the Adirondack Survey for 1880. Verplanck Colvin.

through all hours of the night; he is also frequently seen browsing in the grassy glades of the forest during the afternoon hours, and when I saw the two animals near our cottage in the White Mountains, last summer, it was as late as eight o'clock in the morning. On another occasion I stirred up a deer shortly after midday who was quietly feeding in a forest opening on a mountain side. Dr. Merriam, however, says that it is the habit of Adirondack deer to visit the water at night and retire to the depths of the forest at break of

"Quietly feeding in a forest opening."

day. Unquestionably different individuals are timid to a greater or less degree; that is perfectly plain in their conduct. One will not venture abroad in full daylight, and another has not only been browsing in the open during the greater part of the day, but has joined company with the cows at four o'clock in the afternoon, attracted, perhaps, by the little trough containing salt for the cattle lodged close beside the pasture bars. A glance at a timid deer shows that all his faculties are on the alert: the head is erect, the broad ears are turned in the direction of danger, the eyes intently peer at a single leaf that waggles in a passing zephyr, the nostrils are distended and in motion, and an uneasy fore foot is poised for a run. When the animal is at last satisfied that

Running Deer (from a photograph).

his safety is threatened, the spindlelike legs are raised, there are a few graceful bounds rather than steps over the intervening ferns and lichen-covered stones, and the creature is gone. But in a swift run he covers the ground like an india-rubber ball, touching it only at every sixteen feet maybe.

The beautiful antlers of the deer are shed and renewed each year—the so-called "spike horn," or antlers without any branches, belong to an animal about

a year old. The two-branched horn belongs to a
deer three years old, and so on. Very rarely indeed
a female will develop a spike horn covered with vel-
vet. This velvety covering of the antlers when they

The spike horn.   Antlers four years old.   Antlers three years old.

first appear is a most remarkable part of the development of the horns. I quote in part what Dr. Merriam has to say regarding it : "The new horns of a
deer in the Adirondacks are first seen about the middle of May ; they appear like
soft, dark-colored excrescences
which, as they rapidly elongate,
harden from below upward.
By the time the growth, which
is accomplished in about three
months, is completed, all but
the tips is well ossified ; the
soft, velvetlike skin now begins
to peel off in irregular shreds,
and by the first or middle of

"The skin now begins to peel
off in irregular shreds."

September the horns are generally clean. This vel-
vet does not come away of itself, but the animal rubs

it off against small trees, as if the antlers itched." Judge Caton, of Ottawa, says: "The evidence which I have derived from a great number of observations made through a course of years is conclusive that Nature prompts the animal to denude its antlers of their covering at a certain period of growth, while yet the blood has as free access to it as it ever had."

Four months after the antlers have fully matured they fall off again. The largest and handsomest horns come from middle-aged deer; those with few prongs come from young or very old animals, and sometimes from a very ill-conditioned or sickly one.

The rutting season of the deer is in November; during this month the bucks rush wildly about and

"The bucks fight like troopers."

fight like troopers. As a consequence, that magnificent game park established by the late Austin Corbin in the wild and picturesque region of Sunapee, N. H., has to be closed to all visitors. I am told that it is not safe to meet a deer on the grounds while he is in this pugnacious state of mind; it is not infre-

DEER IN BLUE MOUNTAIN PARK.

ESTATE OF THE LATE AUSTIN CORBIN, NEWPORT, N. H.

One of the largest game parks in the world.

quently the case that he will attack a man and do
some fearful work with horns and sharp hoofs. Indeed, the wild and rampant creature at this time for-
feits all claim to that mild and attractive disposition
which is his usual attribute ; his neck is greatly enlarged, he fights furiously with his fellow bucks, and
sometimes loses his life in a desperate encounter
through the locking of the antlers. When this happens in the wild woods the animals can not separate,
and both miserably perish of exhaustion and starvation. What a strange tragedy of Nature ! Dr. Merriam says that his father possessed a set of locked antlers which he found on the frozen carcasses of two
deer which had perished on the ice in Pine Creek,
N. Y. Audubon also states that he once saw *three*
pairs of antlers interlocked, and remarks upon the
pathetic sight the owners must have made as they
slowly starved in the midst of plenty. But Audubon
did not take into account the fact that exhaustion
shortened the animals' lives, and mercifully, therefore, the period of their starvation.

As a rule, the female deer bears two fawns—one
is quite the exception—and these are born in the
month of May ; they are quick at making use of their
slender, long legs. The little fawn is prettiest when
he is about a month and a half old ; the sides are
spotted with white, the face is delicately graded with

deeper and paler color, and the eyes are unusually large and expressive. The dainty creature is the very embodiment of gracefulness in movement as well as appearance; nothing is more charming than the airiness of his little leaps over the uneven turf, and he is perfectly surefooted; I doubt whether any one ever saw a young deer stumble. He is an inquisitive little animal too, constantly mixing his extreme timidity with an overwhelming curiosity to know what a strange-looking object is made of, and

Female Deer.

trusting to his agile legs to escape if it should prove dangerous. He is also omnivorous, like the goat, and eats anything that comes along. There is a record of one young

A young Fawn.

fawn who was reckless enough to devour a paper of chewing tobacco which happened to come within his reach; but he paid the penalty of his rashness with his life the next day.

Very young fawns bleat like little lambs, and the voice of a doe is a high-pitched and tremulous whistle or squeal. It is said that a buck when he is surprised and frightened utters a sharp, shrill whistle. But he is far from a coward, like the bear, and he runs only when he is persuaded that his horns and hoofs are not equal to the emergency.

If the deer meets a rattlesnake in the woods he considers it a deadly enemy and jumps upon it with "all fours," cutting it to pieces with his sharp hoofs; indeed, he is quite capable of kicking a man into un-

"Swimming across the lake."

consciousness by springing upon him with his sharp-hoofed fore feet. When he is swimming across a lake the rash and unsophisticated hunter who is sufficiently near to grab him by the antlers, does so at the risk of a broken arm, for still the active limbs are ready to inflict a stunning blow. The only way to seize a deer

17

in the water is by the tail—an unreachable member; for the animal is an expert and swift swimmer, who learned the art when he was but three or four months old, and now that he is older his legs are by no means hampered by so light a task.

Contending for half the year with the severities of a hard climate where the mercury frequently drops thirty degrees below zero; chased not infrequently by his deadliest enemy, the panther (*Felis concolor*); hunted night and day by another

Two young Female Deer.

not less deadly enemy, man, the wonder is that the Virginia deer survives in the face of such terrific odds. But, given a fair chance, he holds his own in the wilderness, and with the protection of admirably effective game laws, there is no reason why he should not increase.

In the Adirondacks there have been three ways in common practice of hunting the deer: The first is by shooting him at night, as he feeds on the margin

of the lake, with the aid of a " jack " light—a sort of
reflector lantern which casts all its light ahead from
the bow of a boat in which the hunter is concealed by
the darkness. This method takes advantage of the inordinate curiosity of the animal, and he loses his life
by allowing the mysterious light to approach too
near. The second is by driving—that is, by chasing
him with hounds in daytime, and driving him into the
lake, on the shore of which the sportsman is posted
with his boat, so that he can easily pursue and shoot
him. And the third is by still-hunting—that is, by
following his tracks over the snow in winter and
shooting him after a prolonged chase in his forest
home, perhaps under some fallen tree top where he
has taken refuge. A wounded deer is not usually
followed, but tracked by his prints and blood stains
several hours, or perhaps the next day, after he is
shot. The reason is quite obvious, for experienced
hunters say that a deer will run several miles when
he is severely wounded. Judge Caton says that he
has known of one that ran a mile and a half after he
was shot through both lungs with a 0.44-caliber rifle
ball.

In the State of New Hampshire hunting the deer
by hounds is contrary to law, and in the season allowed for shooting the sportsman must get his deer
the best way he can by means of his gun. This is

the fairest kind of sport, for the deer has an equal chance with the hunter; the latter must still-hunt and prove his skill as a marksman by bringing down his game by a single well-directed shot, or else, with less success, he must make up his mind to follow the tracks of the wounded creature several miles over the snow-clad hills the next day.

Not long ago, a fine deer, weighing one hundred and fifty-four pounds, was shot near my cottage by the "fair-play" means of still-hunting, and my sportsman neighbor,* ever a good shot at a partridge, brought down his game with unerring aim.

The flesh of the deer is the most juicy and palatable of all meats, and it is also the most easily digested. The hide not only makes excellent heavy driving gloves and moccasins, but, when it is well dressed and neatly lined, it makes a handsome chair rug. It is in the best condition in November.

---

* Whose name is James McCann, a true man of the woods, whose knowledge of Nature, from the humblest flower to the giant trees of the forest, including all the animals great and small that live under their shade, I have found to be like an interesting volume—but one not yet published.

CHAPTER XV.

A SEMIANNUAL SLEEPER AND A NIGHTLY PROWLER.

The Woodchuck and Porcupine.

IF one could shake a red and a gray squirrel together in a bag until they merged into one individual with a coat neither red nor gray, then blow the thing up with the bellows into thrice its former size, jam the face together, trim down the ears, enlarge the paws, chop off half the tail, and finish by knocking just half the life out of it, one would have a fair imitation of the woodchuck or marmot (*Arctomys monax*),* that grave and indefatigable old burrower who inhabits the field on every farm in the country—or

---

* His Indian name is Wenusk.

nearly every farm, for his range extends from the Carolinas to Canada, and from the seaboard to Missouri, Iowa, and Minnesota.

The names of this familiar American animal are both significant and appropriate; *Arctomys* comes from the Latin *arcto*, meaning to draw close together, in allusion to the habit of the animal of gathering himself together in a ball for a long winter's nap. The specific *monax* means a monk, also remarkably appropriate, for the animal generally lives quite by himself in the deepest seclusion. As for the plain Yankee name of " woodchuck," whatever may be its serious import, there used to be a legend connected with it of expressive interest, which deserves repetition here.

In olden times—probably the time of Æsop—the lesser animals used to live in one happy country with a judge over them—the dog. One day a rabbit, whose burrow adjoined that of a marmot, complained to the latter that the little rabbits' eyes were continually filled with the dirt which he carelessly threw out of his burrow. However, the marmot paid no heed to the remonstrance, and the rabbit was compelled to appeal to the judge; he immediately sent word to the offender that he must be more careful in the future. But the insolent marmot, notorious for his incivility and indifference, replied to the messenger that he *would chuck* his dirt where he d——d pleased! That settled it; the dog has been hunting for the gross offender ever since, and the name "woodchuck" stuck to the whole tribe.

The general appearance of the animal is not irresistibly attractive; he is grizzly brown over the back and chestnut color beneath; * his body is about thirteen and the tail four inches long; he is so loosely "hung" that apparently he has less bones in his anatomy than a cat. But who does not know the woodchuck well, and what country dog has not soiled his nose in enlarging the endless burrow all to no purpose? He seems to be an encumbrance on the farm, without attraction or interest except for the small boy and the dog.

Not many years ago the farmers of New Hampshire, finding the woodchuck an unmitigated bore, demanded of the State Legislature some measure to relieve them from the impositions of the beast. Alas for the woodchuck! a bounty of ten cents was placed upon his devoted head, and he could venture to stick his whiskers beyond the confines of his burrow in safety only on Sunday, because on that day, if his body fell into the hands of the enemy, the devout Legislature refused to allow the bounty.

---

* Melanistic—that is, black—phases of the woodchuck's coat are not uncommon.

But the chairman of the committee appointed to inquire into the moral status of the woodchuck—Mr. C. R. Corning—was too wise a man not to see the anomalous character of his task. So he turned in a report worthy of a gifted humorist, whose pleasantries are instinct with keen wit and harmless satire. Indeed, he most ingeniously aimed over the woodchuck's shoulder and threw the clown's cap on the farmer's head. So the "beastie" came off easy with the following uncomplimentary comments on his person: "Your committee finds the woodchuck destitute of any interesting qualities. . . . The casual observer is not attracted by the brilliancy of his colors. . . . The family was evidently designed and brought forth under conditions of severe simplicity. . . . The creature's only purpose in venturing forth during the day is to get a good 'lay of the land.' Like the bear, the gait of the thing under consideration is plantigrade; but in order occasionally to exercise its toes, it climbs small trees and shrubs; then, perfectly satisfied that its pedal extremities are in good working trim, it descends to the ground and again resumes its monotonous waddle. The woodchuck, despite its deformities of both mind and body, possesses some of the amenities of a higher civilization. It cleans its face after the manner of a squirrel, and licks its fur after the manner of a cat; your committee is too

wise, however, to be deceived by this purely super-
ficial observance of better habits. . . . The woodchuck is not only a nuisance but a bore; it burrows
beneath the soil and then chuckles to see a mowing
machine, man and all, slump into one of these holes
and disappear!"

Now this most uninteresting animal is a strict
vegetarian; his home is usually on the border of a
fertile field where food is   plenty; this
consists of succulent grasses
and herbs, roots, vege-
tables, and es-
pecially red
clover. Of
the last he
is particular-
ly fond, and
wherever there

"On the border of a fertile field."

is a red-clover field one is pretty sure to see either a
woodchuck or his burrow.

Digging out a woodchuck's hole with the expec-
tation of finding the occupant, is an undertaking too
arduous to find a fit expression in words. The gal-
lery slopes off at an angle of about twenty-three degrees for a length of four feet; then, at a depth of
three—sometimes only two—feet below the surface,
it inclines upward in no settled direction and con-

tinues for about ten feet, but divided perhaps into
two galleries, each of which leads to a circular chamber a foot in diameter; in this there is a snug nest
made of dried grasses, leaves, etc. Here the creature
dwells with his fields of plenty directly over his head,
and one would think that, like the squirrels, when in
the midst of abundance he would set by a store of
good things for the winter; but not at all. He is no
hand at providing for the future;* the very nature of
his food is perishable, and it is a question whether it
would outlast the cold even of a protecting burrow.
Very soon after the autumnal equinox the improvident animal retires to his hole which he has now dug
on the sheltering margin of the wood, and he does
not venture forth again until the arrival of the spring
equinox, which is sometimes coincidental with the so-
called " woodchuck's day." † If the weather is still
too cold to be springlike, his day—which weather-
wise folk always insist is a forerunner of six weeks'
sunshine—will be postponed.

---

* I actually found in Brehm's Life of Animals—a very good
Natural History, by the way—the absurdly incorrect statement
that the woodchuck in the fall occupies himself in collecting
provender for the coming winter!

† In different localities the times of the woodchuck are also
different; farther south, he reappears about the middle of March,
and in the valley of the Connecticut he remains out until November.

He is the most remarkable of all hibernating animals; no other creature sleeps so profoundly or so long. Only the little flying squirrel is at all like him. The gray squirrel sleeps exclusively through the severest part of winter; the chipmunk wakes up to partake of his plentiful stores, and quite frequently takes a peep at the outside world, and the chickaree is abroad all winter except when it is violently cold. But the woodchuck is a sleeper. All the preparation he makes for the cold and foodless winter is an inordinate stuffing of himself with red clover in the latter part of September. He enters his hole, therefore, with excessively sleek and fat sides, and somehow or other lives on his accumulated fat through the long season of ice and snow. In his dormant state the heart action is greatly slackened and respiration is only detected by an instrument designed for the purpose, which must be very delicately adjusted. He can be rolled about like a ball without seeming to be in the slightest way inconvenienced or disturbed; he will awaken in a warm room, but goes to sleep again without an effort. Of course, with warm surroundings and plenty of food he will not sleep as he does in a state of Nature; but his hereditary habit is strong, and he can never be called thoroughly awake in midwinter under the best of circumstances.

In September the woodchuck sits by his hole the perfect image of listlessness; he is as absolutely motionless as a "bump on a log." Possibly he meditates upon the changing aspect of Nature, at any rate he does not move a muscle, and it is doubtful whether his mind works. silently and Approach him never so cautiously and he pops in without a preliminary movement. On one occasion, though, I did actually see him change his position before he disappeared. At first he was upright, then on my nearer approach he dropped horizontally, and when

"The perfect image of listlessness."

I got to within ten feet of him he was gone. Presently I took a harmonicon from my pocket and played softly upon it; being highly susceptible to the sweet influences of music he reappeared at his doorstep, and, with a slight expression of disturbance on his usually dull countenance, eyed me with some curiosity and disapproval. I imagined if he possessed the power of speech he would have said, "This may be quite a clever performance, sir, but on the whole I'd thank you not to disturb my autumn reverie."

When the woodchuck is tamed he is not uninteresting, and there are numerous stories told of his strange habits which are quite amusing. Dr. Kellogg, in the American Naturalist,* tells of a tame marmot he had which was allowed to sit at table with the family in one of the children's chairs. This he did with all possible decorum; but when he smelled the sweet cake and other tempting viands, he forgot his manners and manifested his pleasure by singing a purring kind of a song, during the performance of which his lips and nostrils appeared to be slightly agitated. When the woodchuck is unexpectedly startled by an approaching footstep he utters a sharp, tremulous whistle which reminds one of the agitated voice of the red squirrel.

The female bears from four to six young about the end of April or the first of May; these remain with the mother until the latter part of the summer, when they shift for themselves, digging their own holes and hibernating in the winter quite alone. But one adult woodchuck with his mate inhabits a burrow, not more.

Quite unlike him in both appearance and habits,

---

* *Vide* American Naturalist for June, 1872, vol. vi.

the porcupine (*Erethizon dorsatus*) * nevertheless strongly resembles this meadow burrower in one particular, he is   unqualifiedly stupid, far more   stupid than any other   beast of the

Porcupine on the march.

field. But he can afford to be, for he has few enemies; all creatures except the fisher and the panther let him alone. His fearful quills, which have an awkward way of sticking fast in everything they touch (excepting his own hide), are formidable things

The quills.

to deal with when one wants to seize him by the back. There it is! his back is simply prohibitive; he can carry it with unconcern as slowly as he pleases, for a more effective armor is not to be found outside of the navy!

The porcupine can not even boast of a pleasing countenance. To look one square in the face is to

---

* Another significant name, from ερεθιζω, erethizo, to irritate or provoke, and from *dorsum*, a back. Very wrongly the animal is often called a hedgehog.

THE PORCUPINE.
ERETHIZON DORSATUS.
"His back is simply prohibitive."
Photographed from life by W. Lyman Underwood.

realize the fact that Nature has somehow or other made a botch of it ; its expression is as grotesque as that which characterizes Mr. Tenniel's Jabberwock in Alice in Wonderland. No wonder then, when we surprise him in the wood shed, his uncanny appearance and sluggish movements give us a sort of mental shock. He is like some old, suspicious-looking tramp who is always seen at dusk haunting the outskirts of the farm buildings and scaring people more by his looks than his deeds. When he appears in the *daytime* he is usually lodged high up on the limb

" Nature made a botch of it."

of a tree ; but, as a rule, he remains within his den somewhere beneath a neighboring rocky ledge during the day, and issues forth only at night, when he may be heard gnawing away at the foundations of the old wood shed. He is a nocturnal prowler of the worst kind, doing his deeds of darkness—never anything worse than the gnawing of wood—in the immediate vicinity of the farmhouse. But he sometimes has a bad habit of girdling and thus ruining the forest trees, especially the spruce.

He has a most inordinate appetite for salt, and will devour, in time, the whole floor of the wash shed if he is given the chance, for the simple reason that it has been well seasoned with salt water from the ice-cream freezer. He does not hibernate like the woodchuck, but goes abroad both winter and summer on the coldest and hottest nights. He is also a strict vegetarian, feeding on succulent bark, the foliage and twigs of trees, buds, and beechnuts; but he is always ready to gnaw a house down if it contains a grain of salt; and in the dead of the night he attacks the woodshed door with the vim of a rat and ten times as much assurance, for he can not be driven away with the thundering clatter of old boots and sticks of wood

"He is always ready to gnaw a house down."

against the partition. Nine times in ten he will continue to gnaw until some one opens the door and clubs him away with a respectable-sized piece of cord wood; there is but one thing he heeds, all else fails, that is the firecracker! Of this mysterious invention of a refined civilization he is suspicious; probably the fiery spluttering more than the noise awakens in his dull mind some sense of a danger from which his quills afford no protection, so he moves off.

I once captured one in my wood shed, which had busied himself for several nights previous by altering the contours of the house and the ice-cream freezer. It was night, I had no heart to kill the creature, so he was left till morning under an inverted wash tub. The next day, after furnishing the family with some entertainment by his enticing looks, queer whining noises (he had a shrill cry), and loudly chattering teeth, he was invited to move on with the aid of a shovel and was dispatched by the farm hand. He weighed fully sixteen pounds. His back was broad, his tail flattened and heavy, and his feet naked like a bear's. His claws were large and curved, and these with his peculiar tail showed very plainly that it was not difficult for him to climb a tree. This ponderous tail of his is capable of dealing a tremendous stinging blow laterally; when he hits a dog with it there is an immediate cessation of hostilities, the dog retires with howls of pain, and then, while one devotes one's attention to extracting the quills in his mouth, the porcupine gets away. These quills * under a microscope are minutely rough with a sort of

---

* They are artistically used by the Indians in the Northwest for the decoration of birch-bark boxes, buckskin moccasins, leggings, etc.; often they are dyed a variety of colors.

18

bearded formation which points backward ; thus they continually work deeper into the flesh unless immediately withdrawn. On the porcupine's back they incline backward, and are raised by a special layer of muscle ; but they are never shot from the hide of the creature, as some people ignorantly assert ; the idea is too absurd to receive a moment's notice, yet there are many who persist in believing in it.

The porcupine's nest is sometimes in a hollow log, but oftener under the strewn rocks in the forest. The female bears two—rarely three—young about the first of May ; they are relatively twenty-five times as large as the young of the bear at birth.

"It was not difficult for him to climb a tree."

Photographed from life by
W. Lyman Underwood.

CHAPTER XVI.

SMALL FOLK WITH LIVELY FEET.

The Gray Rabbit, Northern Varying Hare, and the Squirrels.

THE little gray rabbit (*Lepus transitionalis* *) which often goes by the soubriquet of Mollie Cotton-tail, is a most remarkably prolific animal; that is the first thing of interest about the creature. The next thing is, that its favorite food unfortunately is the buds, young shoots, and bark of apple or peach trees—especially those new kinds which one has set out in the orchard. When the moon is shining full over the glittering snow, and the winter night is full of witchery and charm, the æsthetic side of Nature appeals to one's highest and best thoughts. But let the two ears of bunny appear silhouetted against the silvery light, and there is another side of Nature revealed which is not quite so charming. To the artist the picture is not only still beautiful,

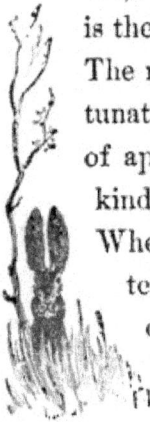

The silhouette of two ears.

---

* Formerly *Lepus sylvaticus.*

but the accent of those two black ears is just one more charm which rounds out the "moonlight monotone" to its fullest perfection.

But to the man who owns the apple orchard, the picture ceases to be beautiful; his eye is obscured with the black whisperings of vengeance, and thinking only of the danger threatening his new trees, he reaches for his gun, and sallies forth into the night with the intention of making a red mark just under the two black ears.

Lepus transitionalis, a rabbit of the woods, is quite as frequently a rabbit of the orchard; and the amount of damage he is capable of doing there is incalculable. He girdles the trees, gnaws the lower twigs, and even climbs into the environing shrubbery to reach the higher ones and denude them of bark and buds. But besides the apple tree, he feeds on the briers, sumachs, hazels,

" Mollie Cottontail."

black birches, hickories, and shrubbery in general which he finds on the roadside and in the garden. He has also other enemies than man, chief among which are the fox, ermine, eagle, and great horned owl; besides these he is subject to attacks by the snowy owl, the larger hawks, the marten, and the mink.

THE GRAY RABBIT.
LEPUS TRANSITIONALIS.
" The moonlight monotone."

The readiness, however, with which he can escape from a pursuer in an open chase saves him from easy destruction. For any swift-footed animal to catch a rabbit on the run is a rare thing; one glance at my sketch of the agile creature's footprints in the snow will show what the nature of his flight is. Evidently it is a series of extraordinary leaps, with

Footprints in the snow.

almost all of the force of propulsion exerted by the hind feet. The hind legs of a rabbit move together as perfectly as if they were joined; the thrust is sudden, and so wide that the hind

His enemy, the Snowy Owl.

legs overlap the fore legs, striking the snow just beyond and outside of them. In watching the leaps of my pet Manx cat, whose hind legs were remarkably long and well developed, I always noticed that he ran like a rabbit, and "doubled up" like those run-

"On the run."

ning horses in Mr. Muybridge's extraordinary photographs; consequently he developed a speed not very far short of that of the wild rabbit.

The gray rabbit burrows in the earth and in the hollows of decaying trees, and winters in quite a snug retreat; often he finds the deserted burrow of the woodchuck quite acceptable for a home. The prolific female bears

"Doubled up."

from four to six young, and she rears from three to four families a year. She lines her nest with soft leaves, grasses, and the fur from her own body. In about thirty days the young rabbits are able to shift for themselves. Like the other small animals the rabbit forms regular

Very young Rabbit.   Young Rabbit.

runways, and in these he is easily trapped. He is so common in some localities that he may be seen day and night skipping through the woods, although, as a rule, he is supposed to be fairly nocturnal in his habits.

His greater relative who lives in the North,
more particularly among the mountains, is called the
American varying hare (*Lepus ameri-
canus virginianus*). This animal is
remarkable for his change of
color; in summer he is a
dark-red brown, and in
winter he is perfectly
white. Regarding the
nature of this change
I must repeat in sub-
stance the opinions ex-

Northern Varying Hare ; summer coat.

pressed by Dr. Merriam and Prof. J. A. Allen.
Dr. Merriam says that when the change occurs
in the fall, the fur lengthens and
blanches, the individual hairs
changing color after the
first fall of
snow. Like
a majority of
the mammals,

In his winter coat.

this hare has two
under and soft kind
parts of the body, and
and stiffer kind which is

kinds of fur : an
which covers all
an upper, longer
scattered through

it. This last, which is blackish in summer, becomes
in the fall white at the tips first, and fades down-

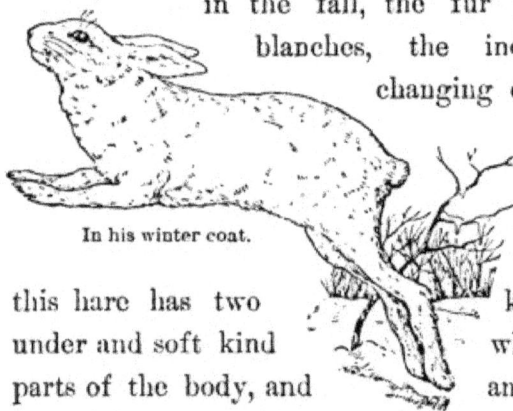

ward. In spring the process is exactly reversed—the exposed portions of the stiff fur become black by the end of March, and while the animal is still white hundreds of the blackish hairs appear scattered over the back, some of which are white in the middle and others white on the tips. In the course of time the white fur loses its vitality, becomes brittle, and is brushed off by the underwood of the forest.

Professor Allen says that while the change from brown to white in the American varying hare is supposed to be largely due to molt, it sometimes appears to take place so suddenly that it is popularly thought to be due in some degree to the blanching of the hair; but the real nature of the change is not precisely agreed upon by naturalists, it is as yet a matter of dispute.

We are at liberty, then, to accept any hypothesis of this remarkable change of color which seems most reasonable; and "who shall decide when doctors disagree?"

In summer this varying hare feeds upon leaves, buds, berries, and succulent herbs and grasses. In winter he has to content himself with the bark of young poplars, birches, willows, and such berries as the snow may leave uncovered; often, too, he gets what he can in the vicinity of the farm by prowling around at night. But his enemies are plenty—the same as those of the gray rabbit—and he is ever on the alert for an unexpected attack.

He follows definite paths of his own making, like the gray rabbit, but unlike him he does not inhabit a burrow. His nest is the rather uncertain shelter of a fallen tree, or the covering of some hollowed log. In this he remains most of the day and ventures out for food at night. The female bears from four to six young in the latter part of May.

This hare is very common in the North country, and is sought in the early winter by sportsmen, who consider his flesh the best of eating. Many of the animals find their way to the Boston market, and a well-conditioned one, which may weigh from four to nearly five pounds, makes a savory stew fit for the table of an epicure. In parts of northern Maine, New Hampshire, and Vermont, this hare is abundant; and in the vicinity of Nipigon, Ontario, during the fall and winter, many of the poor things are killed in the night by the passing trains of the Canadian Pacific Railroad. Mr. G. S. Miller, Jr., writing of the varying hare which he found plentiful just north of Lake Superior, says that one was taken on the 5th of October at Peninsular Harbor, the winter pelage of which was just beginning to appear on the ears and buttocks; but on certain others taken two weeks later the winter coat was nearly complete.

Inhabiting the same wood with the varying hare, but far more active than he is in every motion of the body, the sauciest scamp in the forest glade, and a notorious little villain for stealing a march on birds' nests, the red squirrel, or chickaree (*Sciurus hudsonicus hudsonicus, Sciurus hudsonius* of Allen), is perhaps the most familiar phase of wild life in the forest or on the highway. But some of his tricks and manners are not thoroughly well known.

He is a perfect nuisance to the trapper, as he continually springs the traps set for martens and minks, and quite often gets caught him-

The Red Squirrel.

self. But his hide is not worth a cent, so the trapper is disgusted. As for his habit of robbing birds' nests, that is fairly well known by every one who lives in the country in June. Last spring a pair of robins built their nest close to my cottage in a butternut tree, around the trunk of which I had built a rustic arbor, and all went on without disturbance until the young birds were hatched, when, late one afternoon, a red squirrel appeared, and in a very unconcerned way began to ascend the tree ostensibly to see how the

butternuts were getting on. I knew very well what
he was after, however, and noticed how slyly he
sprang to one of the lower limbs which led in the direction of the nest. No sooner had he done this than
the father bird, who was at least thirty yards away
in a maple tree, made for him, and immediately there
was a great commotion among the butternut leaves.
In the midst of it the mother bird appeared with a
hard-shelled bug in her mouth, which she dropped,
and I heard it rattle down the arbor roof. Up and
down, in and out among the leaves the birds chased
the little scamp, and still he tried to elude the sharp
bills, but vainly; it was perfectly plain that the
birds had the best of it, and that bunny's agility was
no match for such a terrific winged onslaught. He
fled at last in great confusion; but the birds did not
desist, and in his frantic attempts to defend himself
he lost his hold and fell from limb to limb, until he
landed on the arbor roof. Before he could recover
himself the robins were at him again, and it was a
running fight all the way to the neighboring pasture
bars, where the birds gave up the chase and returned
to their tree. It was amusing directly after to see
the male bird station himself like a sentinel in a
maple that adjoined the butternut. But it was just
as well, for he had to defend the nest a third time
before the fledglings were flown.

The red squirrel is also a thief. He frequently has an encounter with a chipmunk at the latter's door-step, and I have caught him in the act of stealing the stores of his more provi-

The Chipmunk scolding.

dent cousin. A chipmunk has his hole just beneath a pine tree outside of my garden fence, and most of the time the little creature travels back and forth between this and the kitch-en door with his cheeks (he has large pouches in them) stuffed full of prov-ender. Every once in a while there is a squabble under the pine tree, and I well know what it means —the red squirrel is there, thieving, per-haps. He is a good deal of a bully, and when it suits his fancy he attacks the hoards of the field mouse, which are care-fully tucked away under some de-caying stump, and, utterly regard-less of the agitation he is creating among the proprietors, who survey

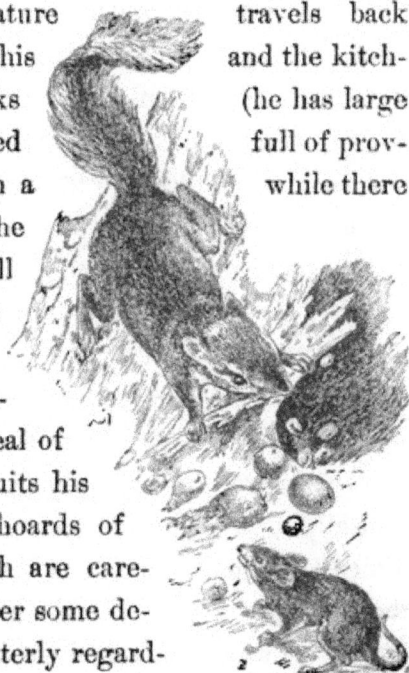

"He attacks the hoards of the field mouse."

his deeds with squealing disapproval, tears their home asunder and eats their stores before their eyes, contemptuously scattering the beechnut shells and the half-gnawed acorns over the snow under their very noses.

In the autumn I have seen him among the topmost branches of a butternut shaking the nuts down and nipping at the stems of the more tenacious ones. One day last October I heard the continuous thump, thump, thump of the dropping nuts, and stepping out of my studio to see why they should fall when there was not a breath of air stirring, caught him at his work; then I took a mean advantage of his industry, and sent the children out to gather the nuts. He surveyed their actions with the disapproval of a much-abused but helpless owner, and scolded most vociferously. He is extraordinarily busy all through the months of September and October, and the stores of beechnuts, butternuts, acorns, and hazels he gathers would, if they were all piled together, astonish one beyond measure. Why, when he gathers so much for himself, he must needs steal from his neighbors, it is difficult to understand. He has the keenest sense of the exact locality of a nut, and I am certain that he is led to attack the nest of a mouse more by his nostrils than his eyes. The keenness of his scent is proved by a bit of calculation which he did one win-

ter in my closed-up cottage. A bushel basket filled
with butternuts was placed close against the surbase
in one of the rooms adjoining the attic. There was
no possible way for the squirrel either to enter or see
inside the room; yet he smelled those nuts, and entering the attic, gnawed his way through the partition, and entered the room through the surbase exactly at a point *opposite the center* of the basket!

His food in winter, though, is not wholly confined
to nuts; he eats the buds of the maple, oak, and
birch, and any seeds or
dried berries which he
can find. He attacks the
farmer's corn barn, and,
unless the corner posts
are well protected with
slippery tin, effects an entrance and carries off the
grain. A careful examina-
tion of the kernel shows

"He will deftly handle a cone."

that he eats the *germ* and leaves the rest. In the
evergreen forest he will deftly handle a pine cone,
and inverting it cut away scale after scale and devour
the seeds hidden between; in the same manner he
demolishes a spruce cone. He does not hibernate,
but keeps thus busy all winter long.

He is an excellent swimmer, and crosses the pond

in midsummer when it is too troublesome to go
around.   But I notice that he avoids the colder water
of the river.   The forest he claims for his own, and
any one who dares to disturb its quiet and seclusion
he hails with a storm of chattering, whistling invec-
tive, the meaning of which may be fairly summed up
into two words—"Get out!"   His squeaky voice, not
very different in tone and quality

"The wrathful creature jerks fearfully."

from the raspings of an old violin in the hands of
an amateur, strikes harshly upon the ear.   All the
while the body of the wrathful creature jerks fearfully from head to tail!

The nest of the red squirrel is usually in the hole
of a tree; sometimes, farther South, it is constructed
of soft, shreddy bark, and hidden in the thick upper
branches of the spruce or the red cedar; in this case
it is spherical, and the opening is near the bottom.
The female bears from four to six young about the
first of April.   She has few enemies to fear, the
owl and the hawk being the only ones of serious consequence.

The red squirrel is reddish brown throughout the summer; but twice in the year he sheds his hair, and during the winter his aspect is much duller, and the red is not nearly so pronounced. Beneath he is white, and there is a dark line where this white meets the red on the sides. In winter the white is toned with brown gray, and the dark dividing line disappears.

The chipmunk (*Tamias listerii*, formerly *Tamias striatus*) is the red squirrel's cousin; but they have little to do with each other, and avoid all unnecessary meetings. A Western species of this genus, *Tamias neglectus*,* which is common in northern Michigan, Wisconsin, and Minnesota, is distinguished by the four stripes on its back instead of the three which characterize the more Eastern species *striatus*. The stripes, except the black, dorsal one, are white in the middle and bordered on either side with black. This Western chipmunk only hibernates when his food supply is cut off by the snow; he will remain out when the temperature is as low as 15°. North Bay, Lake Nipissing, Canada, is the most easterly point where he has been found.

The Chipmunk.

---

* Formerly *Tamias quadrivitatus.*

The Eastern chipmunk takes to his winter bed in the ground as soon as the cold and frosty nights of October come, and reappears again in March or April. He is not a profound sleeper, however, and often wakes up to "eat a bit." His abundant store of nuts,* seeds, corn, and buckwheat is tucked away underground where the red squirrel can not get at it, and he passes the winter in peace and plenty, only popping his nose above ground when the weather is warm, to make sure that the world still "wags on."

The tail of this little fellow is insignificant, his body is much less athletic in its lines than that of the red squirrel, and in every way he shows himself *not* a climber. If he is scared in the forest, and takes refuge in a maple, he clings helplessly to the bark somewhere about fifteen feet above the ground, and waits without a motion for the danger to pass, descending again spirally.

He is not very timid, but I do not know that he is very easily domesticated. He is constantly about in my garden while I am at work there; he feeds on the sunflower seeds in the autumn while I stand within five feet of him, and the children frequently feed him with crusts of bread and cake at a respectful but

---

* It is a matter of some surprise to me that he cares for the clumsy big butternut; but he often tackles one, and even carries it to his hole. As a rule, however, he prefers seeds to nuts.

19

moderate distance.   He also hangs around the kitchen way, and not infrequently enters the door in search of a few fallen crumbs.   On all his excursions to his burrow, not far from the front gate, he pouches appears with his cheek so stuffed out that his eyes are half closed, but on his return his physiognomy has resumed its normal proportions.

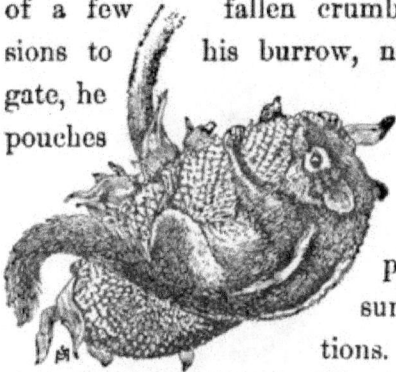

"He feeds on the sunflower seeds."

He is quite the opposite of the red squirrel in one respect—he is quiet.   Rarely he raises his voice above a scolding murmur, which sounds like *chip-chip-ur-r-r,   chip-.-r-r-r-r.*

The nest of the chipmunk is in a hollow chamber about as large as a cocoanut at the end of a tunnel about two feet long, and sixteen inches below the surface of the ground.   The female bears from four to six young about the latter part of April.

"The children frequently feed him with crusts of bread."

One of the prettiest of our squirrels is the little, soft-eyed, velvet-coated flying squirrel (*Sciuropterus*

CHIPMUNK.

TAMIAS LISTERII.

" He is the red squirrel's
cousin."

volans volans, Sciuropterus volucella, Geoffroy);
but he is out only after sunset, and does not often
appear on the highway. His color is a
brownish gray, and his skin is so loosely adjusted to his body that he
can spread it out in a wide ex-
panse and slide through the
air from tree to tree on
a flying leap of fully
fifty feet. It is said
that on extra occasions
he can stretch this dis-
tance to one hundred

The Flying Squirrel.

and fifty feet; but I am confident of the fact that
this is merely a fall, after the fashion of a parachute.
Even the red squirrel can fall a matter of thirty feet
with no inconvenience to his anat-

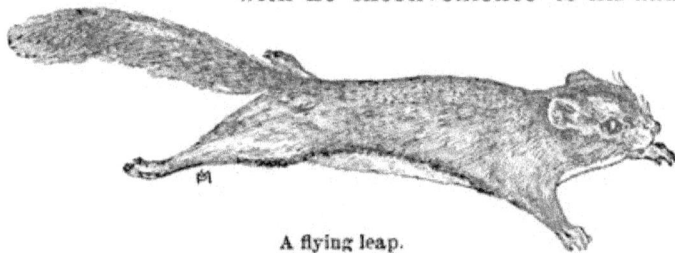

A flying leap.

omy, and there is no doubt but that a flying squirrel
can sail a hundred feet or so through the air with all
the semblance of a long leap, but in reality the distance covered *laterally* is not so very great. This

little creature is common all over the country, from the East to the West, as far as the plains. I have often seen him in Holderness, N. H., and he is common at Profile Lake, Franconia Notch, N. H.

The nest of the flying squirrel is in a hole in a tree. The female bears from four to six young about the first of April or later. When captured and tamed the little ones make most charming pets.

Next to the woodchuck, the flying squirrel is one of the most profound sleepers of all hibernating animals. He retires to his nest early in November, and does not reappear until the latter part of March.

The big relative of the red squirrel—an animal made of coarser clay—

The Gray Squirrel.

is the Northern gray squirrel (*Sciurus carolinensis leucotis*). This active fellow, familiar in many of the city parks, hibernates only when the weather is extremely cold, and then for no great length of time. So long as the mercury will stand above 16° the gray squirrel will venture out in the cold; but when it drops below that, and the chances of food on the snow-covered ground are scarce, he seeks the warmth and seclusion of his nest in the hollow of a tree, and stays there until the weather moderates. He is undoubtedly the most easily tamed of all our squirrels, and it takes only a small amount of patient waiting and quiet behavior to gain his confidence in the wild wood. A pocketful of nuts is one of the surest means of establishing an intimate acquaintance with him; and if one is careful not to move suddenly and noisily, he will approach and take a nut from the

Music!

hand. He is also susceptible to the charms of music, which may be amply proved by carrying a small music-box in the pocket for his especial entertainment.

The nest of the gray squirrel is usually built in the crotch of a tree or in the hollow of a partly decayed limb. The female bears from three to five helpless little ones,

The Black Squirrel.

which are at first quite blind and hairless; they remain with the mother two months. Sometimes, farther South, the female will raise two litters in a year. The black squirrel is *not* a different species; his darker fur is simply a phase or variation of the animal's more common condition in life — this dark color, in fact, is simply a case of melanism.

It is very important in the study of wild life that we should recognize the exact relationship of the animals, just as it is of like importance that we should know the affinities of plants. Without this knowledge one studies Nature at an immense disadvantage. It is a good beginning, for instance, to learn that we have really but two species of the fox in this country, and that there is an affinity between the little sundew plant and the larger pitcher plant. At present, even the botanists do not fully recognize the relationship between these two insect-catching characters of the vegetable world; but they will surely do so some time in the future.

As for the animal world, naturalists have not yet done with it, or at least with that part of it which is on this side of the Atlantic. Our black squirrel and gray squirrel are one species; our weasels are none of them the ermine; our black bear and cinnamon bear are two of a kind—*Ursus americanus*—and our Northern and Southern green snakes are unrelated excepting in color.

To tell the truth, naturalists are still busily "sorting things out," and several of them say that they have not yet nearly finished; but I have given the latest facts as I found them, and it is to be hoped

PRAIRIE DOGS.

darker fur is simply a phase or variation of the ani-

for the long wait — of perhaps four minutes. It was nothing more nor less than a huge brown grasshopper, nearly as long as the small bird himself. Again was the camera used as a halting-place, and again did she fly on my hand. Hungry though the little fellow may have been, he was unable to swallow so large a mouthful, and he dropped the grasshopper into my partly closed hand. Unfortunately I had just pressed the bulb and was therefore unable to take a photograph of the interesting proceeding that followed.

Quite naturally the mother bird was anxious that so bountiful a supply of food should not be wasted, and she stood on my thumb and bending down, so that her head was *inside* my hand, extricated the prize. Then she proceeded to break it into pieces of suitable size, and with these she fed her quivering and impatient little offspring. During the morning I secured a few more photographs of these interesting birds, and then returning the youngster to the bush whence I had taken him, I left the pair in possession of their hillside estate.

latest facts as I found them, and it is to be hoped
that some of the last *names* to come in will not leave
us before this book becomes ancient history! But
then—*Tempvs est omnibus rebus.*

INDEX.

281

THE END.

FAMILIAR FLOWERS OF FIELD AND GARDEN.

By F. SCHUYLER MATHEWS. Illustrated with 200 Drawings by the Author, and containing an elaborate Index showing at a glance the botanical and popular names, family, color, locality, environment, and time of bloom of several hundred flowers. 12mo. Library Edition, cloth, $1.75; Pocket Edition, flexible covers, $2.25.

In this convenient and useful volume the flowers which one finds in the fields are identified, illustrated, and described in familiar language. Their connection with garden flowers is made clear. Particular attention is drawn to the beautiful ones which have come under cultivation, and, as the title indicates, the book furnishes a ready guide to a knowledge of wild and cultivated flowers alike.

"I have examined Mr. Mathews's little book upon 'Familiar Flowers of Field and Garden,' and I have pleasure in commending the accuracy and beauty of the drawings and the freshness of the text. We have long needed some botany from the hand of an artist, who sees form and color without the formality of the scientist. The book deserves a reputation."—*L. H. Bailey, Professor of Horticulture, Cornell University.*

"I am much pleased with your 'Familiar Flowers of Field and Garden.' It is a useful and handsomely prepared handbook, and the elaborate index is an especially valuable part of it. Taken in connection with the many careful drawings, it would seem as though your little volume thoroughly covers its subject."—*Louis Prang.*

"The author describes in a most interesting and charming manner many familiar wild and cultivated plants, enlivening his remarks by crisp epigrams, and rendering identification of the subjects described simple by means of some two hundred drawings from Nature, made by his own pen. . . . The book will do much to more fully acquaint the reader with those plants of field and garden treated upon with which he may be but partly familiar, and go a long way toward correcting many popular errors existing in the matter of colors of their flowers, a subject to which Mr. Mathews has devoted much attention, and on which he is now a recognized authority in the trade."—*New York Florists' Exchange.*

"A book of much value and interest, admirably arranged for the student and the lover of flowers. . . . The text is full of compact information, well selected and interestingly presented. . . . It seems to us to be a most attractive handbook of its kind."—*New York Sun.*

"A delightful book and very useful. Its language is plain and familiar, and the illustrations are dainty works of art. It is just the book for those who want to be familiar with the well-known flowers, those that grow in the cultivated gardens as well as those that blossom in the fields."—*Newark Daily Advertiser.*

"Seasonable and valuable. The young botanist and the lover of flowers, who have only studied from Nature, will be greatly aided by this work."—*Pittsburg Post.*

"Charmingly written, and to any one who loves the flowers— and who does not?— will prove no less fascinating than instructive. It will open up in the garden and the fields a new world full of curiosity and delight, and invest them with a new interest in his sight."—*Christian Work.*

"One need not be deeply read in floral lore to be interested in what Mr. Mathews has written, and the more proficient one is therein the greater his satisfaction is likely to be."—*New York Mail and Express.*

"Mr. F. Schuyler Mathews's careful description and graceful drawings of our 'Familiar Flowers of Field and Garden' are fitted to make them familiar even to those who have not before made their acquaintance."—*New York Evening Post.*

New York: D. APPLETON & CO., 72 Fifth Avenue.

FAMILIAR FEATURES OF THE ROADSIDE.

By F. SCHUYLER MATHEWS, author of "Familiar Flowers of Field and Garden," "Familiar Trees and their Leaves," etc. With 130 Illustrations by the Author. 12mo. Cloth, $1.75.

"A faithful guide-book for our roadsides. . . . Can be unhesitatingly commended for summer strolls."—*New York Evening Post.*

"One who rides, drives, or walks into the country, particularly in these days of bicycling, will find this book an invaluable and incessant source of elevating amusement."—*Philadelphia Press.*

"Deserves to be the guide-book *par excellence* of the familiar wayside. . . . His book, taken as a whole, is a treasure."—*New York Times.*

"An admirable book for Nature lovers to take with them to the country, for it reveals in a delightful way many mysteries of insect and floral life, and comes as an exquisite refreshment and welcome instructor."—*Boston Times.*

"A delightful study of Nature in her manifold forms. . . . Take this trip on the road with Mr. Mathews, for he is a very entertaining lecturer, and has personal acquaintance with buds and flowers."—*Minneapolis Journal.*

"The book is certainly a charming one for all lovers of Nature, and can but inspire a love of the waysides for any into whose hands it shall come."—*Boston Saturday Evening Gazette.*

"It is such a book as will direct the attention of its readers to those features of everyday life with which they are often unacquainted, because they have never stopped to give them attention."—*Jersey City Evening Journal.*

"A beautiful book, and as interesting and instructive as it is beautiful. . . . The lessons of the book are enforced so pleasingly as to make every page fascinating."—*Chicago Inter-Ocean.*

"A book to carry through one's summer wanderings, to quicken one's appreciation of common beauties."—*Philadelphia Public Ledger.*

"A book that ought to be in the satchel of every one who takes a vacation; and even stay-at-homes will find a new interest in their surroundings through its perusal."—*Chicago Advance.*

"A thoroughly charming book alike for the amateur naturalist and the lover of out-door life."—*Boston Beacon.*

"It is impossible to express the fascination of such a book as this."—*New York Commercial Advertiser.*

"The book is one for people who are fond of the country. It is not merely instructive, but is suggestive and stimulating, and helps people to use their own eyes to advantage."—*Brooklyn Eagle.*

"An introduction to a boundless world for which every lover of Nature will be deeply grateful—luminous, learned, appreciative. . . . A valuable and delightful book."—*New Haven Leader.*

"The book is most interesting and instructive, and will be found to impart useful knowledge in a most entertaining manner."—*Hartford Post.*

D. APPLETON AND COMPANY, NEW YORK.

*B*IRD-LIFE. *A Guide to the Study of our Common Birds.* By FRANK M. CHAPMAN, Assistant Curator of Mammalogy and Ornithology, American Museum of Natural History ; Author of " Handbook of Birds of Eastern North America." With 75 full-page Plates and numerous Text Drawings by Ernest Seton Thompson. 12mo. Cloth, $1.75.

" ' Bird-Life ' is different from other books. It deals with birds that are familiar, or half familiar ; it interests the ignorant reader at once, and it makes the relations between birds and men seem more intimate. The economic value of birds will be better appreciated after reading this book."—*Boston Herald.*

" Contains more information about birds, in the same space, attractively as well as concisely stated, than can be found in any other book with which we are acquainted. . . . A delightful, valuable, instructive, entertaining, beautiful book."—*Brooklyn Standard-Union.*

" Most heartily can ' Bird-Life' be commended. It is by a practical ornithologist, but it is simple and comprehensible. It is compact, pointed, clear. . . . The work is perfectly reliable. . . . The author uses every line to give information. A straightforward and very compact guide-book to bird-land."—*Hartford Post.*

" An intelligent consideration of the book will add to the reader's pleasure in his walks in field and wood, quicken his ear, make him hear and see things which before went unnoticed. . . . Gives the student an introduction to ornithology, which places him on the threshold of the entrance to the innermost circles of bird-life."—*Boston Times.*

" Mr. Chapman's book ought to be as greatly in demand in the average household as a history of one's country."—*Providence Journal.*

" The illustrations are undoubtedly the best bird drawings ever produced in America."—*Recreation.*

" A comprehensive book, one that is sufficient for all the ordinary needs of the amateur ornithologist. It is satisfactory in every detail, and arranged with a care and method that will draw praise from the highest sources. Every lover of outdoor life will find this book a delightful companion and an invaluable aid."—*Buffalo Enquirer.*

" A volume exceptionally well adapted to the requirements of people who wish to study common birds in the simplest and most profitable manner possible. . . . As a readily intelligible and authoritative guide this manual has qualities that will commend it at once to the attention of the discerning student."—*Boston Beacon.*

" Such a study as every intelligent reader will desire to make, even the busiest of them. . . . The author is in every way fitted for the task he has taken, and his book abounds in its facts of value, and they are pleasingly and gracefully told."—*Chicago Inter-Ocean.*

" An interesting mass of data collected through years of study and observation. . . . While accurate from a scientific point of view, it makes delightful reading for those who will soon be among the flowers and the fields."—*Philadelphia Inquirer.*

D. APPLETON AND COMPANY, NEW YORK.

www.ingramcontent.com/pod-product-compliance
Lightning Source LLC
Chambersburg PA
CBHW021107270326
41929CB00009B/767